# Preface

This little book is offered to its readers in the hope that some of you will find its reflections helpful as you make your way through the thickets and dry places of the wilderness that is called a human life. That wilderness is getting more and more wild, it seems, as the days and years of our tempestuous times advance; and what there may once have been of widely accepted—if not always observed—models and patterns for the living of that life have now fallen into question and disarray. Lives have become more and more individual as each person, mistrusting the maps and trails, arbitrarily selects one out of the many offered and thus serves as his or her own scout. What opportunity there is for the development of individual talents and visions is sometimes lost in the crisis of self-confidence to which excessive individualism can lead.

This guidebook may be no more than another individual chart; yet it may have the value of setting the entire journey in the largest possible context, that of a view of the cosmic and immortal meaning of each individual human life here and now. The language and background patterns of time and destiny used here are derived, if they are drawn from any particular source at all, from the theosophical tradition. These are not presented with any dogmatic motive, but rather because that is a tradition I have found especially helpful in dealing with such ultimate matters. Readers are entirely free, of course, to take what they find of use from this book and leave the rest.

May you have a good trip through this book, and through your life!

—R.S.E.

# The Pilgrim Self

Traveling the Path from Life to Life

# The Pilgrim Self

## Traveling the Path from Life to Life

### Robert Ellwood

A publication supported by
THE KERN FOUNDATION

## Quest Books
Theosophical Publishing House

Wheaton, Illinois ♦ Madras, India

The Theosophical Publishing House
P.O. Box 270
Wheaton, IL 60189-0270

A publication of the Theosophical Publishing House,
a department of the Theosophical Society in America

**Library of Congress Cataloging-in-Publication Data**

Ellwood, Robert S.
      The pilgrim self : traveling the path from life to life / Robert
Ellwood. — 1st Quest ed.
            p.    cm.
      "A publication supported by the Kern Foundation."
      "Quest books."
      ISBN 0-8356-0739-9
      1. Spiritual life.    2. Theosophy.    I. Title.
BL624.E465  1996
299'.934—dc20                                                96-8902
                                                                      CIP

The following publisher has generously given permission to use an
extended quotation from a copyrighted work:
   From THE EXPERIENCE OF NO-SELF by Bernadette Roberts,
   ©1982. Reprinted by arrangement with Shambhala Publications,
   Inc., 300 Massachusetts Avenue, Boston, MA 02115.

                  6    5    4    3    2    1    *    96    97    98    99    01    02

Book design by Joyce Knutsen

Printed in the United States of America

# Contents

PREFACE                                                          ix

1   A Series of Sunrises                                          1

2   Chinks of Eternity                                           21

3   Wake of Splendor: Infancy and Childhood                      45

4   Questing and Nesting:
    Adolescence and Young Adulthood                              65

5   The Sun in Strength:
    The Years of Early Creativity                                87

6   The Demons and Delights of Midday:
    Middle Age                                                  105

7   Sunset and Evening Star:
    The Beauty of Old Age                                       121

8   Many Meetings, Many Partings:
    Circling Paths through Death and Life                       135

9   Always Beginning, Always Coming Home                        155

NOTES                                                           161

## A Series of Sunrises

Take your average night.

It begins with the setting of the sun. Red and gold fill the west, then all too soon they crumble into gray. The sky goes deep blue, then darker still. The friendly trees, so recently gay and green, turn somber-black as specters. Waters in friendly birdbaths and ponds become inky and infinite as the deeps of space and time. The horizon closes round nearer than shouting distance, save for a glitter of lights signaling the universe is still there—lights from houses and roads, and on clear nights from the diamond tiaras and necklaces of stars lavished across the heavens by the queen of night.

You yourself are probably within, fixing and eating dinner. This may be a simple or a complex matter. Perhaps a pizza comes your way through the gloaming, or you throw a frozen dinner into the microwave. Or perhaps you make something special in the cheery kitchen as darkness gathers without—something interesting with eggs, peppers, mushrooms, and onions; a baked potato with sour cream and chives; carrots seasoned with sage; and a big salad complete with artichoke hearts tossed in oil and wine vinegar.

However you go, during this sacred meal—sacred as are all meals—the dining table becomes a circle of light, a place of transformation where life turns to life as foodstuffs become human. Whether you talk with family or friends as you dine, or you read alone or watch TV, you feast upon words with ideas behind them as well as upon victuals. The dining circle is a hermetic circle, a circle of secrets and magical change around you, as the shadows outside lengthen to infinite.

Then after dinner you may sit in the living room for a while, perhaps in front of a lively fire, reading, or absorbing a movie on the screen. Either way, you are slipping more and more into a realm of symbols. Words, pictures, sounds—they are little flat things in themselves, small and thinner than a moth's wings on paper or on the airwaves or the screen. Yet they have the power to fire the neurons of your brain till you envision love on a riverboat or palaces in Tibet; and you feel all the emotions in Shakespeare—but wholly in your mind, as you lean back almost too comfortably in that easy chair. It is the hour of symbols: They gather like fairies under the moon when day is done, and they lodge with you till morning.

Not that noon is any less a time of symbols. But morning symbols are the symbols of human exchange: money, numbers, invoices, status-tokens—like the make of one's car or the thickness of one's carpet. Those of the night are subtly different; they do not frame the world so much as they make worlds. Night symbols render one an observer, who is also divinely able to taste the sweet and bitter fruits of the tree of life, then withdraw to the innermost fields of Eden.

It is time for bed. Clothes are removed; there is a moment of Edenic nudity, then the softest of fabrics are draped over you. The lights are dimmed; night moves in very close; the clean warmth of sheets and blankets comes round, as in the crib.

Do the symbols then cease their revels? Hardly. Round and round they wheel: phantasms with feelings clipped to them—of those you love and those you hate, plans for tomorrow, insistent sexual fantasies, the story you have been telling yourself for years that no one but you knows—all in the mind, all symbols; for they are all like animated statues, turning on and off by the swift action of mind, and if you look you see behind each one another symbol of deeper meaning, and behind it another, and so on and on into caverns of mind measureless to humankind.

You fall asleep, and now the symbols come fully into their own, in the hour toward which the night has been building. For in dream they alone are real. Now scenes of flying and falling, of strange adventures, of pursuit by monsters where almost no one can hear you scream, of giddy laughter and ecstatic visions—all slide into consciousness.

Finally, deep sleep without dreams arrives. You are simply one with the universe, and there falls no separating veil of thought. You revert, as it were, to the realm of nature and its secrets only; and the soft throbbings of your body are one with the silent dances of the atoms and galaxies, and that is enough.

Then you awake, and the castles of sunrise are building outside and casting their gold across the floor. As you quietly struggle back to consciousness, you may see a final figment of the dream in the corner by the chest of drawers, as though to say farewell, for you are still between the worlds. But victory is now with the light; you stretch and feel the body, stiff, almost numb, slowly gathering itself. Then, suddenly, you are "*I*, of such-and-such a name." *I* must get up, *I* need to brush my teeth, *I* have to do this and that work today.

You arise, and take your stand on the floor. You remove the garments of night, and put on those which declare your identity in terms of the symbols of the outer world: suit, uniform, office dress, blue collar, the studied casualness of the student.

You grab breakfast. You glance at the newspaper, a symbolic act of reimmersion into the stream of outer life, with all its hooks: that murder trial everyone's talking about, that trouble over in Transmontania. The minority leader charged . . . the home team might win the pennant . . . the industrial averages fell five points. . . . You lay the newspaper aside, and it is already almost forgotten, its transitional function performed. Time to go.

You step out, and you're in the sunlight for just a moment before the car door slams shut. There's always a moment of tension as, radio blaring to cover it, you merge into the traffic of street or freeway. Am I going fast enough? Too fast for my lane? Then you're in, and it's like a great dance; you almost sing as you weave in and out. . . . That afternoon, when you get home, perhaps you take a moment to check the mail and then, before supper, to just sit a spell, holding it all together, your day and your life. . . .

And so it goes, your day and all your days run together. A series of sunrises, with night following behind them—each night a little death, each sunrise a minor birth . . . linked together by a single secret, the secret of who you really are.

Who are you? Who am I? You know, unless you are totally insane or the world is considerably odder than we think, that you woke up in that bed as the same person who had gone to sleep there. You know this because you are aware of continuity in the same physical body, and because you possess a string of memories associated with life in that body going back to early childhood. Along with them, you have a set of attitudes connected to the "I" feeling of this body and memory chain—I'm a person who does this and doesn't do that, who likes this and not that, who believes one thing and not another. Finally, you know that somewhere amidst all of this resides the real "I," an ego or will, that can make decisions and set a course for its life.

You may be aware, if you have read much psychology, that there are those who scoff at such notions. The idea of a will or an ego, they would say, is an illusion; what we think of as free choices, like our notional selves, are just the products of irrational drives and stimuli. We know not why we act the way we do, or why we are who we are, but we make the best of it by calling it all a choice.

Perhaps on some ultimate level ordinary ideas of will and ego are to be transcended, although for the sake of discovering unimaginably greater grades of freedom than we now know, not for the self's diminishment. But at present we live in a world of provisional reality, in which selfhood must be provisionally accepted and worked with, for it is all we ordinarily know—except for rare flashes of mystical insight—about who or what we are.

What, then, is a self? After the physical body, it is, first of all, a chain of memories. Memories are rough instruments, to be sure, for defining a person. Try remembering everything that happened to you when you were eight years old, or ten. If you are like me, you can recall only a few incidents—a trip to the beach, a day in school, an accident; and chances are those sometimes inconsequential-seeming memories are selected not so much because of their own importance, but rather because they have a role, symbolic or otherwise, in the stories we now tell ourselves about who we are and how we got that way. We are also increasingly becoming aware of false memories—that it is quite possible to "remember" something clearly and vividly and then find irrefutably that it never happened. False memories can be implanted in several ways: by repeated suggestion from others, including hypnotic; by badly "needing" a memory to confirm a certain belief; by confusing dreams or fantasies with waking experience; by conflating several separate episodes into one. But memories—true and false—have a part in making a self.

There is another self-maker too, one even more indefinable—the sense of the core-essence of a person. How do we recall an important other, a friend or loved one? Usually a certain look, a twinkle, or cast of the head will be what emblazons itself on our minds. If we see a picture that has that look, that certain smile, we say, "This is really Miranda or Uncle Joe"—even though the person may, in fact, only occasionally display that memorable mark of what you know to be her or his true self.

It is a mystery. And it applies to you, too. You know better than anyone when you are "being yourself" and when you are "putting on," going through the roles and rituals so often demanded of us by the world of uniforms, and no less by the world of dreams. You may somehow know what your core-essence is, though you would be hard put to express it in words. You apprehend that real self as a kind of center, a conscious point moving through some space and a lot of time—or perhaps it is the other way around; it is a still point past which the universal array of symbols strung out in space and time is streaming by like multicolored fish in an endless sea. However that may be, we are that center of conscious awareness surrounded by symbols bidding for attention, trying to say, "Listen to my message. Hear what I'm really all about. Here's what the world is really all about."

Day and night. Light as a symbol, dark as a symbol. Both symbols climbing up the great chain of being all the way to the Face of God . . . and beyond: the Light Inexpressible, the Divine Dark of the mystics' God above God. The hermetic circle of the dining table. The climes and cultures, the laughs and tears of printed page and silver screen. The unimaginable wonder of the night sky. And, the next day, money and the make of one's car. No less real than the Divine Dark. Just the Divine Dark in another disguise, the Light Inexpressible breaking in sidewise.

For everything we see, hear, smell, taste or touch is a symbol of more than itself. It represents where it came from. It is an ambassador of the kind of society that made it. More subtly, it bespeaks the plane of reality on which we're living. Finally, it is a veiled but tangible manifestation of Ultimate Reality itself . . . incomprehensible, whether we call it Divine Light or Divine Dark, whether we say it is too bright for our eyes or too dark for our sight. For every being, however seemingly superficial, stems from and participates in all levels of reality down to the ultimate. If God is everywhere, She/He is in every object in the universe, including ourselves.

You're driving and you come to a traffic light. First off, it's a sign saying without words to stop or go. But it's more than that; it's a symbol of modern technology and government, and their power to order our lives in such matters as starting and stopping in traffic; no such lights were known to the Middle Ages, and not even the most autocratic medieval despot attempted the lowly task of regulating traffic. The traffic light is a fruit of the era of electricity, the internal combustion engine, and smooth paved thoroughfares, and so— more than a sign—it is also a symbol of that whole world. And insofar as it exists, it is a symbol of Being Itself, of the ultimate Light and the ultimate Dark, of God. The theologian Paul Tillich has said that a symbol participates in that which it symbolizes.

We are surrounded by symbols; everything is a symbol, and symbol upon symbol. The chain of symbols, in fact, weaving in and out of each other seems to be endless; perhaps this is a clue that reality itself is endless. Symbols are illusions, in that they are not—or not only—what they seem; they are also significant, for they teach that reality all around is more than it seems, and more than what can be taken in from just one angle of vision. Helena Blavatsky in *The Secret Doctrine,* a basic theosophical text, wrote:

> From the standpoint of the highest metaphysics, the whole Universe, gods included, is an illusion; but the illusion of him who is in himself an illusion differs on every plane of consciousness; and we have no more right to dogmatize about the possible nature of the perceptive faculties of an Ego on, say, the sixth plane, than we have to identify our perceptions with, or make them a standard for, those of an ant, in *its* mode of consciousness.[1]

This may lead to a presentiment that one's own self is not just an observer of symbols, but is itself a symbol intertwined with all the others and participating in something larger than itself. But what?

When you sit down at the end of the day, when you think about the novel of your own life together with your private worlds of dream and story, does it ever seem that these may all be only parts of a larger story, in which many currents flow together to make up a longer drama, like many streams combining into a mighty river moving toward the ocean? Does even the day after day shuffling of workaday symbols occasionally become as the moving of pieces on an immense chessboard, its edges and four corners who knows where?

Somehow, in some dusty inward nook or cranny of the mind, we question whether all that this life means and is can be explained only by what happens between birth and death. Do all the symbols around us play on such a small stage? What about the symbols that appear and appeal to us as they leap off the pages of the books we read, or from the television screen? Or those that romp as provocatively and absurdly through our dreams as those of *Alice in Wonderland*? When we look at the things we choose to have around us in our homes, how do we read their significations? Why do we like baroque objects better than Victorian, say, or prefer listening to modern musicals over grand opera? Taste, one might suppose—taste good, bad, or personal—but that, like any other answer that can be given in words, evades the question of Why? that lies behind every answer. As in science, as in every enterprise of the human mind, questions come first and last, answers come only provisionally and in-between.

Those reflective moments give rise to deep questions that lie behind these symbols and our varied attachments to them. Most people have asked—to no one in particular, unless to God—Why was I born in the time I was, in the century I was, and not another? Why was I born in this place, this country, this world, this particular universe, and not another? Why to this family, with its particular social and economic standing, its ethnic and racial background, and not another? Why this body, with its certain smile, and perhaps its all-too-familiar disabilities, and not another?

For some, such questions are beyond answering, like the question of why we are conscious in the first place. For Theosophy, as for Hinduism and Buddhism, the beginnings of answers can be found in the concepts of infinite life, and in karma. These teachings tell us that we have lived not one but countless lives, and that the dynamic which leads from one to the circumstances of the next is karma, or cause and effect, on the spiritual and mental as well as physical levels. The workings of karma are very subtle, and to comprehend all the factors contributing to even a single human birth would be far beyond the scope of all but the most extraordinarily advanced intelligence. Yet the concept, if looked at with sufficient sophistication, can provide a tool for approaching the meaning of our own lives.

Helena Blavatsky spoke of the individual Self as the Pilgrim, on a tremendous journey outward from the Halls of Light which are our true home, and back to them again. During the course of this epic progression the Pilgrim is to learn, to experience, to grow, and to return to its original purity enhanced by all it has learned of the conflict and compassion incumbent upon individual selfhood. Particular experiences of the Pilgrim can call for particular sequels in the impersonal wisdom of the karmic field. We may need to complete certain lessons, or finish certain relationships, or even experience temporal rewards; and above all we are drawn to particular settings by deep webworks of affinity.

We can be sure that all of us who are flourishing on Earth in the late twentieth or early twenty-first centuries have been led to take birth in this specific time and place because, beneath all our apparent differences, we have an affinity—or should one say a compulsive need?—for the human life of this time and place. Something in each of us, in you and me, resonates, whether through appeal or dread, to its pace, its symbols, its potentials and its catastrophes. Appalling as it may seem, each of us has needs that can only be met by our living in the same century as two world wars, technological advancement from horse and buggy to moon rocket, and tremendous population explosion. On a lesser scale, we need to live as neighbors to certain people also sentenced for life to these dreadful and wondrous times, and are fated to more intimate connections with the times as parent, spouse, or child to a smaller number of others of the same ilk. We were born with the possibility that we could die at Auschwitz, or be among the greatly increasing numbers who will live past ninety. We are destined to watch on a silver screen phantasmagorias beyond the dreams of medieval wizards, and to fly from cities on the broad Missouri to the golden sands of the Pacific in a hundredth of the time it took by covered wagon just a hundred years before. And a fifth of us are hungry almost every night, and see children's bellies swell for want of the simplest food. All this we witness, ponder in our hearts, and pound down to seed-size, seeds we then take with us beyond the circles of time and space to germinate, and finally to bloom as flowers of strange new colors in a different and, one hopes, better world far in the future.

For now, however, we need to work through the particular inner and outer problems of our age, and for now, none other; we have people on this troubled, overpopulated planet with whom we need to share deep dreams and the depths of life, and with whom we need to settle scores and play scores together. You could perhaps have been born a super-intelligent sea-worm on a planet around Procyon, or even an earthling of the eighteenth or twenty-fifth century, but your affinities have led you to this time and place at this point in your pilgrimage, and that much—and it is much—you and I have in common with all others who are here.

We are often tempted to think we deserve a better world than this one with all its horrible cruelty, hatred, and injustice that is as present now at the end of the twentieth century as ever. Yet if we are honest with ourselves, we are likely to realize that these things are not wholly alien to us. They are part of our nature too; we also have thoughts and impulses—perhaps strong even if repressed—toward cruelty, greed, and selfish disregard of others near and far. Few of us can say we are not where we belong, even if it is not where we would like to be; and those few perhaps are here out of an unselfish desire to help.

Indeed, in the last analysis you and I and all the others here have made this world what it is from the inside out, have made it as an outward symbol of our individual and collective states of consciousness because in its beauty and horror alike it is a world we both deserve and need. Think of our earlier image of self as a center with symbols whirling by. In Theosophy, consciousness is a fundamental reality, and symbols are the first and last tools of consciousness. Worlds and human lives are ultimately the outward expression of states of consciousness, formed in interaction with matter—the shapes come together as like seeks like and makes them.

Yet this one time and one world is not all that we are. Our sense of alienation from the world around us is also a reality bearing its own truth. Sometimes there is a half-articulated feeling deep inside us that this particular planet on which we find ourselves is not, and ought not to be, our real and final home. This feeling needs also to be heard. For though it is easy to deceive ourselves about our everyday virtues, there is something within us that *is* better than this oft-sordid place— something we brought with us from the Light of the Beginning, and which is and shall ever be like a star far, far above the clouds of this globe, and which this world's pollution can never touch.

That spark of eternal, unkindled light is the Pilgrim who has seen many times and many worlds, who has learned from them all yet shaken off the dust of each from her or his feet, and has remained unspotted. But with the Pilgrim, like the pack on her or his back, is the burden of those long journeys, the karmic weights ever lost and gained that tilt the pilgrimage now this way, now that.

If we are Pilgrims who have seen the sun rise in many aeons and over many different worlds, then we are indeed not *just* of this world at this particular point in its history. Though we have been drawn to it by powerful affinities, we also have potential for more. We can consciously disidentify with it save to serve it with compassion. This is what all great religions teach us to do—to be *in* the world but not *of* it, to labor in it but to be unattached to the worldly fruits of the labor.

The wisdom and wonder tradition that Theosophy represents teaches that life is a Path along which glints of the eternal glory may often be glimpsed. This is the glory from which the pilgrimage came and to which it shall return—and which is always enveloping it, beneath the surfaces of the hard world. For that which is eternal can never be absent, only hidden from the sight of clouded eyes. This tradition also teaches that life on the Path is a series of initiations that are openings, through which more and more can be seen by those who prepare their eyes to see.

What is an initiation? Life is a series of asking questions and a series of initiations—the two go together. As we have seen, the questions have no end, for all the

answers turn into deeper questions. The child asks
what it is like to be adult, and in time is initiated into
adulthood through a series of experiences that expand
awareness until adulthood is encompassed. But adults
also have questions. Initiations may include words, but
they are different from instruction, which is primar-
ily verbal. An initiation, instead, is an experience—
natural or intentional—that brings us into an aware-
ness that can be gained only through proper prepara-
tion and through total, multisensory experience, not
by words alone.

That is why we began these considerations with
day turning into night and the shadows lengthening,
for every night is surely a minor initiatory experience.
To go home and go to bed is different from going to a
classroom, but it can be just as transformative if not
more so. For night changes perception through all the
senses; the hermetic circle of the table, the book or the
screen, and above all sliding into dreams, change con-
sciousness as profoundly as almost any drug. How
many animals are quite different in temperament,
almost appearing a different species at night from that
of day! Only because we experience this change so fre-
quently are we often inured to it, and do not see in
every Day the Light Inexpressible, and every Night the
Divine Dark. But day and night are the most common
of the great cycles by which, according to Theosophy
and many teachings, the universe turns as it revolves
between manifestation and unmanifestation. The ini-
tiation of each night is a rehearsal for the great sleep,
the turning we call death.

The basic initiatory experience at the heart of all
great spiritual rites and transitions is modeled on death

and rebirth. In religion and spirituality, one dies and is reborn in many ways—baptism, the Sweat Lodge and the Vision Quest, manhood and womanhood rites. . . . An initiation is a death to one kind of life, and a birth to another in which one is more widely aware, and in significant rapport with a larger environment—just as nightly sleep is death to day, merging with the larger cosmos of the dance of atoms and galaxies, and reawakening to the next sun.

But significantly, initiations can take hold only when one is ready, and that may be a matter of time and growth, as well as of intentional, personal preparation through such means as study and self-discipline. Though the child may ask what it is like to be an adult, the verbal answers one can take in as a child do not add up to wisdom about adulthood. That comes only after—through a series of biological and social initiations—she or he dies to the life of a child and is reborn as an adult, a person with wider horizons and wider capabilities on both the biological and social levels.

As already indicated, there are two kinds of initiations. Natural initiations are those we pass through just because we are human beings transiting human life: birth, puberty, adulthood, parenthood, old age, death. Various cultures also design social initiations, often in conjunction with natural initiations. These help individuals go through the natural ones in ways compatible with the society's values. They put natural transitions in a sacred context, such as those initiating young women and men into adulthood. These initiations are often programmed to bring out very dramatically the death and rebirth aspects of the rite, with candidates perhaps being sealed in a lodge, or even semiburied at the heart of the rite; the candidates may at this time expect to see visions and hear the voices of gods as signs of expanding awareness.

Social initiations can also be individual, undertaken voluntarily or in response to a personal divine call. People in the past voluntarily undertook the initiations of the ancient "mystery religions," such as those of Eleusis or Isis, as today they become initiated into lodges, fraternities, religious orders, priesthoods, or discipleships. Like all initiations, the scenarios may offer the candidate powerful sensory and subjective experiences which help awaken new kinds of knowing, and aid one to see individual life in the context of newly appreciated spiritual environments.

In addition to natural and social initiations, Theosophy, like most spiritual traditions, affirms what may be called inner initiations. These follow no obvious biological or social program but have a dynamic of their own—or rather, a dynamic linked to one's past and present web of interactions with the larger environment in ways too subtle to be seen save with the eye of wisdom. In this kind of initiation, one passes through inner death and rebirth experiences, and realizes inner awakenings to broader horizons and new dimensions of one's material and spiritual environments. One may, of course, stimulate such initiations through practices like prayer and meditation which make one especially accessible to them; yet they usually happen with seeming spontaneity. When one is ready and open, the initiation occurs in its own way. In classic spiritual writing, initiations are represented as transitions between such stages of inner growth as Illumination, the Dark Night of the Soul, and the Unitive state. These stages, summarized in modern times in the writings of Evelyn Underhill, will be looked at more precisely a little later.

A single life viewed in this way is a path within the Path. The great Path, the Path from Light to Light on a journey through countless worlds, planes, and aeons, has its highs and lows, its initiations, its crises and their resolutions, all perhaps on a scale larger than can be fully grasped in one lifetime. But that lifetime trip from birth to death also has its initiations and its vicissitudes, its play with the world of symbols and its hints of the timeless glory in ways appropriate to each of its stages, even as the single day with which we began is a short initiatory path that can be a miniature of the lifelong path, while also being an important segment of it; and that lifetime path can be an important, if relatively brief, segment of deeper initiations and still longer Paths, measured by the durations of ages, worlds, and universes, whose trails wind down finally from heights hidden by the bright clouds of eternity, and reascend back into them.

That is the premise of this book—that one's life is an initiatory path and is also part of a longer Path. The inner feeling that one has had an ultimate birth of which all our other births have been recapitulations is to be trusted. If in deep memory you keep alive an ultimate sunrise of which those that occur each morning are souvenirs, and you treasure that memory in the midst of ordinary days, this book is written for you. In it, we will observe a single life, and see how the path wends its way through it—like a stream through fields and forests—from infancy to old age. But all along the way we will discover reminders, if we have eyes to see and ears to hear, that we are are here only on a visit;

and while there is necessary business to attend to in this world, our appointment here must be set against a wider canvas, and be seen as part of a longer journey than we are now able to fully understand.

In early childhood one may have fantasies or memories of the primal Light and of other times and worlds. In high adulthood those timeless moments come when the rushing of the world stops and a certain frame is saved for eternity; or it becomes a window through which the eternity of the Light shines into the world in a way that you or I can receive it: as a moment of love or joy, in a thing of beauty, or for an instant when the turning symbols configure into a pattern that catches for our eyes the meaning of the whole. With age, for those well prepared, comes a peaceful sense of rounding off a cycle, and the knowledge that it's all right because one has done it all before.

Let us now turn to these chinks of eternity in time.

# Chinks of Eternity

E ternal meanings, meanings relevant to the nature of our long-term progress on the path, can be perceived in the ordinary-seeming events of everyday life.

When you think back on your life thus far, what are the moments you remember most clearly? There are, of course, the conventional memories: the successes, the graduations, the weddings, the births, the tragic or disastrous occasions we would like to forget but cannot. But right alongside of them there are, I suspect, vivid yet inexplicable memories of "ordinary" days: a fifth-grade morning in school, a teen-age afternoon at the beach or overnight with a friend, a young-adult party or workday, an ordinary long summer evening in the park with small children.

Why do we remember these days? Are they perhaps not just happenstance, but symbols of something profoundly important? I suspect they are such symbols, and their message is that all days are good days. Not in the sense of being happy rather than unhappy, in the everyday meanings of the words, but in the sense that they are memorable. Because the ordinary days can be remembered they do not die. Because they do not die they are part of eternity. Because they are part of eternity they have eternal meaning, and that means they are good—even the seeming defeats and horrible occasions—because they fit, like somber-hued pieces in a puzzle, into a pattern which eventuates in the triumph of light and joy. The divine is found in the ordinary, and in the end the divine wins.

That is not to say that everything that happens, good or bad, is predestined. We, and all centers of consciousness throughout the deeps of space and time, have free will, and can decide for good or ill. According to traditional teachings, destiny set by cause and effect, or karma, lays down the conditions of life—where and when one is born, whether high or low, rich or poor, and in what family—but how one then responds to those conditions, how one lives that life in the circumstances with which one is presented, is an individual response. The subsequent decisions are yours. Karma deals you the hand; how you play it is up to you.

But often the choices are not clear. Or the demands of ego triumph over those of compassion, even though it is compassion that recognizes the true nature of reality, that of interconnected heart and soul. The evil which we feel in the bad hours and moments of our lives is not necessary, but is mandated by our own choices now or in the past—perhaps the remote past—or by the choices of others which impinge upon us. Occasionally, as is hinted by traditional stories of satans and demons, we may suffer from the malevolence of greater beings than ourselves that are able to spiritually blight nations, or even worlds, years or generations. But most often the fault is ultimately our own, for even if there are outside malevolences, how we receive them is still up to us. The good news, however, is that it all works together for good in the end, or more accurately, is *now* together for good in the end.

Now, consider *how* we remember the episodes in our lives. Isn't it interesting that we see the past less as moving, like TV news or a movie, than as a series of stills? We have this scene or that face etched in our mind, like a painting or a timeless moment from myth. The scenes are rich, linked to feelings—the joyous, sad, angry, or fearful feeling of the moment back then, with perhaps an added-in note of poignancy, nostalgia, wistfulness, yearning, or regret as keen as grief or joy, as the past is contemplated from a later vantage-point. The remembered episodes are full of symbols. And they seem always there, as though the creations of time are not momentary constructs to be destroyed as soon as they are made, but eternal realities through which we are moving, animating one moment after another, like a spotlight turning over a landscape, illumining now one feature and now another. Yet we know the other moments are still there, in the dark like toys that have been put away but that still exist in memory, and which live at the bottom of a mysterious space-time toy box. Who knows, perhaps their moment in the light may come round again.

Time and memory, then, are strange, always changing and always there. Some memories we may wish were not always there, and could be destroyed forever. Some may give us far more pain than anything else. But it is better to remember in joy. To remember even the pain in joy. Not by dishonestly denying the pain, or pretending it was something else. Nothing is ever gained spiritually through dishonesty or denial.

Rather, what we are after is affirming the good that was always there behind the pain even back then; the beauty that still reposed in the sky, the trees, the forms and faces of that day, however terribly the clouds and the shadows fell over them; the good that inheres in the original and true nature or purpose of anything, from human to virus, however bent it may have become; the good that is the vitality and energy of life even when suffering; the good that anything is insofar as it exists, and is not nothingness.

It is said that we learn through pain and suffering. No doubt true. But it is even more true that we learn through joy. For in joy we touch the heart of the world; in pain we encounter only the guardians at the threshold. That is why Christianity has always said that the resurrection is a deeper and greater mystery than the crucifixion, and Buddhism that the Buddha only reached the calm joy of full enlightenment after experiencing and giving up both the pleasures of self-indulgence and the pain of extreme self-denial.

On the Path, that which teaches is what helps us to let go, to release our grip, to lighten our load and move on. Pain can do this. Illness can force us to get free of indulgences and addictions; psychological pain can lead us to reassess bad relationships or misdirected ambitions; material loss can help us find other grounds for worldly happiness than our possessions. But it is tricky; pain can also drive one into a black hole of self-pity and chronic despair that is worse than any other false attachment, and it can finally reduce the mind to a dullness that is at an opposite pole from the acute discrimination on which spiritual liberty is grounded.

Yet all joy is a teacher, though not all pleasure; for pleasure, like pain, can befuddle, causing us to confuse our goals and narrow our horizons. But real joy, which is precisely the joy that comes when we lose the burden of self-consciousness, plunges into the joy at the heart of the universe and so is like it, adamantine and unlimited. Joy may dive in through a particular opening: the light of that jewel, the loveliness of those eyes, the contours of this moment in time. But these are only the vehicles. A well-known Zen saying is that when a finger is pointing at the moon, we look not at the finger but at the object to which it is directed; in the same way, when we are caught by an aperture to the joy at the heart, we are attracted not to it but through it. The experience of rapture or love is not for its sake alone, but is for the sake of the world, and that beyond the world.

What makes any experience a teacher is that it opens a window into the center of things, into the way things really are all the time. It may be an opening to the deep heart of joy; it may be a glimpse of the snarling guardians of that treasure—pain and anguish; they, too, are teachers if they succeed in showing us what must be left behind with them before we pass on. So it is with the memories of earlier times: of childhood punishment or sickness, of a bad day in school, a disappointing romance. Or of happy times. Or of a few days that seem just along for the ride. But they are all important because they are all lenses. The hours of our days and the days of our years are moving images of eternal realities. Nothing is without meaning; nothing however small fails to reflect some angle on the divine mind, or shine a flashlight on how things really are. Each episode is a chink of eternity. Large and small, inner and outer, all reflect each other. The clouds and rain of an atmospheric thunder storm can be reflected in our inward moods, and when we finally win through to joy it is like the limpid air and iridescent rainbow of a storm's end. So does each chink of eternity reflect a facet of the larger story of our life and lives: the journey to eternity.

In the first chapter of this book we spoke of the Pilgrimage of selves through the worlds of space and time, and of how episodes that stick in memory may relate to other stops along the way, or to particular problems or opportunities to be dealt with in this life. Now I would like to consider how the incidents of our lives ultimately refract, into our days and nights, the final goal, the eternal Halls of Light.

The Halls of Light are, in fact, here and now, shining through everything we see, solid in everything we feel, even while stumbling at night. All realities of our lives are soul-sized: every night a reminder of the Dark Night of the Soul; every sunrise of Eternity. For if Eternity is unconditioned reality, it is everywhere and there is nowhere it is not. It is only our thoughts that make spiritual things distant; it is only in our fearful and abstract fantasies that enlightenment is a remote goal and heaven further away than the Andromeda galaxy when, in fact, they are nearer than our hands and feet. As Zen has always emphasized, you will never be enlightened any time other than the present, and Nirvana—unconditioned reality, Suchness, union with God—is here and now. We are Buddhas, enlightened beings, today—as we wash dishes, walk down the street, do our work and our play, if we but catch on to that timeless truth.

In light of this realization, we must understand that the concept of spiritual growth through life is a tricky matter. Certainly there are changes, and we are not the same at the end as at the beginning. But the idea that we should keep on "growing" from infancy to the grave can easily become an obsession which does not consort well with the real rhythms of life. As the archetypal psychologist James Hillman has pointed out, that notion may be just a projection onto the rest of life of the experience of childhood and adolescence, when growth in all sorts of ways—physically, emotionally, mentally—is indeed a pervasive and ongoing reality. But adulthood is significantly different: not properly a time of stagnation, to be sure, but a time which finds its truest meaning less in perpetuating ego-centered "growth" than in giving and returning.

For Hillman, human consciousness is a labyrinthian cavern of images with neither beginning nor end, though the light may shift from one to another. This, I would say from our point of view, is profoundly true of experience within time itself, though there is a path into time and out of time, and the light shining over the cave of infinite images is the light of that same eternity. For Hillman's archetypal psychology, the great human temptation then is to see, or rather force, into a heroic ego concerned with conquering and overcoming, certain of these images or "gods."

As heroes we "ascend," but at the cost of not fulfilling potential for multiplicity and diversity, and ultimately our conquest is futile. Wholeness is not that sort of sterile ego integrity, but is a self at home with a multiplicity of imaginal presentations, each to be received with joy in its own time. It envisions a human life as the embodiment of a sequence of many "gods."

But "spiritual growth," as a project of the conquering imperial ego, is, as Hillman has suggested, merely a fixation on the maturation process of childhood and youth projected onto the rest of life. In those early years we really are growing and changing biologically, emotionally, in every way. But when those processes stop in their juvenile form at adulthood, the perspective on what change and growth in one means ought to subtly shift as well. To continue trying to be a growing child or adolescent, like any clinging to a time of life that has come and gone, now produces only twisted results. Fixation on "growth" at this stage entails being inflated with only one of the "gods," doubtless the most conquest-oriented of them, at the expense of all the potentialities encased in the others. True adult life, Hillman says, is not progressing "to" anything; it is rather, ideally, the subtly and infinitely varied rounds of experience afforded by fulfilled relationships and fertility on both the psychic and biological planes. To be sure, there can still be development and positive change, but it will now work in a different way and in harmony with different psycho-biological rhythms.

In this perspective the experience of all the stages of life are valuable, none to be seen merely as a prelude to something else or as something to be "conquered" by something else. Instead, each offers the supreme model of a complete, fulfilled spiritual life—one might say a kind of sainthood—for that age and stage; how close we come to it is our measure for that time, and we should not measure the spiritual quality of one stage of life against the model for another.

Look at it this way: There may be an infinite number of worlds in the universe, representing every possible variation of conditioned reality, and in infinite time they may go through every possible stage of manifestation. Some may be of incredible beauty, others veritable hell-worlds, still others like ours, more or less in between. But they are all linked by one commonality: They are all expressions of the One, shaped by the karmic requirements of countless beings, and they have as their inmost nature Oneness and are subject to the workings of Universal Law. As *The Secret Doctrine* puts it,

> The Universe is worked and *guided,* from *within outwards.* As above, so it is below, as in heaven, so on earth; and man, the microcosm and miniature copy of the macrocosm, is the living witness to this Universal Law and to the mode of its action.

And again:

> From Gods to men, from Worlds to atoms, from a Star to a rush-light, from the Sun to the vital heat of the meanest organic being—the world of Form and Existence is an immense chain, the links of which are all connected.

In every world, in every stage of life, in every situation, then, lies hidden meaning, purpose, and a way to the Center. No world, no situation is so hellish that it is not part of the Unity, and therefore not connected to the Halls of Light along a Path which, though it may be torturous, can be followed by any Pilgrim prepared to set foot thereon.

If that is true of worlds and aeons, it is also true of our own lives, our own particular links in the Great Chain. At each point the Path leaves for the Center; in each, indeed, the Center is visible through the things of that time and place. The small child's perception of beauty in a handful of sand on a sunlit beach, or the adolescent's anguish at the end of a relationship, are reflections of the Way as real as St. John of the Cross's Dark Night of the Soul, or William Blake's vision in *Auguries of Innocence:*

> To see a World in a Grain of Sand
> And a Heaven in a Wild Flower,
> Hold Infinity in the palm of your hand
> And Eternity in a hour.

Perhaps many of us have experienced every once in a while—in the midst of ordinary days and events—that strange sense of the timelessness that lies behind time and, even more strangely, is one with time, that can now and again break through the events of time, making them seem as they truly are, at once transient and immortal. The poet Rupert Brooke captured such a moment in the midst of a casual afternoon tea with laughing friends. All went on normally—

> Till suddenly, and otherwhence,
> I looked upon your innocence.
> For lifted clear and still and strange
> From the dark woven flow of change
> Under a vast and starless sky
> I saw the immortal moment lie.

One instant I, an instant, knew
As God knows all. And it and you
I, above Time, oh, blind! could see
In witless immortality.

I saw the marble cup; the tea,
Hung on the air, an amber stream;
I saw the fire's unglittering gleam,
The painted flame, the frozen smoke.
No more the flooding lamplight broke
On flying eyes and lips and hair;
But lay, but slept unbroken there,
On stiller flesh, and body breathless,
And lips and laughter stayed and deathless,
And words on which no silence grew.
Light was more alive than you.

For suddenly, and otherwhence,
I looked on your magnificence.
I saw the stillness and the light,
And you, august, immortal, white,
Holy and strange; and every glint
Posture and jest and thought and tint
Freed from the mask of transiency,
Immote, immortal . . . [1]

Yet for all the timeless glories along the way, a path does imply movement, and somewhere to come from and go to. I prefer to call it "Walking the Path" rather than "Spiritual Growth." Certainly, as on any walk, there is change of both scenery and muscular tone over the course of a life. We can enlarge our capacity for love, for peace of mind, for self-understanding, and for awareness of reality beyond our objects of desire. We can see new things, or like Rupert Brooke, the same things in a new way. We can even grow in awareness of deep joy.

However, just as paths can meander, our steps do not advance in an even, straight-line progression. We have all known older people whose faces and eyes are like quiet clear candles, who give peace to all who come near them. But we have probably also known older people who are bitter, angry, possessed of an inner sourness that seems to distort the very features of the face. Most distressing of all, we may have seen people of sterling character and spiritual purity who have turned into much less in old age, due to disease and depression or dementia that seem to be beyond their control. These disturbing observations belie any facile idea that one life is necessarily an occasion of visible, clear-cut spiritual growth.

But Walking the Path is a little different. It does not imply, as does the model of growth, a change from one irreversible state to another, as in the way the woman will never be the girl again. Walking is just going from one place to another. Perhaps you go around in circles and see the same sights a second time, though never in quite the same way as the first. One will be in sun, another in shade; one will be in the first flush of energy, another in a more tired mood. But you keep on Walking.

As you walk you may come to awareness of past sins, mistakes, mischances when there was a vast foreshortening of vision down the trail. Some things you now deeply regret may carry consequences you will have to live with the rest of this life-pilgrimage, in terms of your life-situation, physical or emotional health, or torturous memories that will not die. There are hours of bitter regret, of tears and rage. But those ills were made in the arena of cause and effect; karma prevails.

Even as it does, there may also be to the eye of memory stars of light still shining amid the darkest passages toward the present day. Fog and starry night arising out of the past are the great challenge, and greatest opportunity, for clean awareness. Then past is past, gone by; you keep on Walking. The trail runs on, and rises finally even above the stars. There will be a new dawn, a new sunrise, new lives. You keep on Walking.

So it is that spirituality is never a status you attain or a possession you acquire, like a college degree or a merit badge. It is, at rock bottom, simply a capacity for *awareness,* and this is something that can be enhanced as you mature from childhood to adulthood—as learning occurs slowly and sometimes painfully by education and example, about the control of feelings and the thoughts behind them, as demanded by civilization. With difficulty, you learn that awareness is needed of what you are saying, doing, and thinking. Finally, you may gain the ability to see your life and thoughts from the vantage point of an observer, as though viewing them on a screen. This is Walking the Path —not just to walk, but as on any journey, to see what is there; and on this Walk one walks with bright and watchful eyes through oneself, as well as through the fields and forests around one.

The first kind of awareness is Self-awareness—to be able to know what is going on in your own life, to be able to feel your sorrows and to monitor your responses, to take note of anger, fear, or self-pity. These feelings may be self-centered, but to be aware of them from the observer's perch is the first step beyond self on this Walk. But the change is now in awareness, not automatic improvement. Martin Luther said that we are *simul peccator, simul justus,* always sinners yet also always returning to right relations with God by faith. Rightly understood, there is a profound truth here. It is a great mistake to think that one is ever perfect, unable to sin or to make a wrong move. If you think you are a saint, or a bodhisattva, that is a pretty sure sign you are not one. Really aware people are too busy relating to God and other people through love to keep taking their own spiritual temperature or worrying about their spiritual status. Self-awareness means recognizing the faults that are inevitably there, yet also learning why you do the things you wish you would not do, and striving to get around them by seeing your life in a larger perspective, in respect of its divine as well as human nature. You realize that self-centeredness is not just a recipe for unhappiness, it is also founded on an illusion about how the universe works.

For the next kind of awareness after Self-awareness is Other-awareness, starting with the realization that no part of our life is truly lived alone, separate from others, from the rest of the universe. A person who even begins, if only intuitively, to understand that the universe is not self-centered but interrelated will begin to really sense as if they were her or his own, the joys and sorrows of others. The Bhagavad-Gita says:

> Who burns with the bliss
> And suffers the sorrow
> Of every creature
> Within his own heart,
> Making his own

Each bliss and each sorrow;
Him I hold highest
Of all the yogis.[2]

Real compassion then is based on reality, for nothing in the universe exists of itself, but as a part of something larger: the quark in the atom, the atom in the molecule, the molecule in the cell, the cell in the body, the body in the world, and up through the solar system, the galaxy, the universe. All that we do affects a larger system, and the larger affects the smaller, and our bodies, as microcosms of the universe, are in profound linkage with all.

This leads to the third kind of awareness, which combines Self- and Other-awareness, and might be called Reality-awareness. It is awareness of the diamond-like reality behind all these filters, inner and outer, which shines through them. It is the calm center in your own mind into which flows cosmic deep joy. Reality-awareness takes seriously everything that is real—the faults and tragedies of everyday life, the glory behind it. But this kind of awareness is an experience, not an irreversible "state," which comes at the most splendid moments of the Walk—though Reality-awareness can be wondrously prolonged, and sometimes is. To be Reality-aware means to be aware of the largest possible dimensions of reality. One cannot be blind to any clue to that dimension: Blake's flower or grain of sand, the eyes of another.

Now on the Path you ask, What clues may appear, and what doors of perception may open in various acts of the drama of life? The five stages of the spiritual life, as presented by Evelyn Underhill in her classic book

*Mysticism,*[3] are intended to suggest stages of experience that a person seriously trying to walk a spiritual Path, or expand awareness, is likely to encounter. They are Awakening, Preparation or Purgation, Illumination, the Dark Night of the Soul, and the Unitive state. The first two parallel and focus on what I have called Self-awareness, for it is necessary to know yourself very deeply before you can proceed to know others and God aright. The third, Illumination, parallels Other-awareness for it is, among other things, a time of the great development of sympathetic joy and love. The fourth, the Dark Night, is a return again to Self-awareness on a far deeper level than before; it prepares you for the most profound, and also simplest state, the Unitive, which is one and the same as Reality-awareness.

Since I am describing these stages, and correlating them with the natural periods of life upon which this book is based, I would like to comment on Underhill's stages as a schema. It would be very unfortunate if one were to think of these five as a sort of checklist, through which you progress and then come out the other end as a certified mystic. It is far from being similar to passing through grades in school or ranks in the military. As Underhill acknowledges, one does not necessarily go through them in sequence at all. Many great souls, she says, have skipped a stage, or worked on two simultaneously, or even become a great saint by staying with only one and mastering it to perfection.

We need to realize that the spiritual life is far more akin to an art than a science, or even an acquired skill such as swimming. All true artists know that, while talent and incessant practice may both be indispensable, their ability in the last analysis is a gift over which they have only limited control, and that in some profound sense they are eternal beginners. All painters, poets, and performers have "off" days when they never seem to get it quite right, and others when inexplicably the colors, the words, or the music seem to flow brilliantly and almost effortlessly. In the same way, the greatest adepts of the spiritual life, if they are honest, talk of "dry" periods, and days when they almost give up in doubt and despair. Yet there are other times when the presence of God is nearer than hands and feet, and an inner divine joy is quietly bubbling from sun to sun. No schema can, nor should, try to cover all these individual nuances and variations. At best it can serve only as a road map in relation to an actual journey.

Three or four people following the same map and attempting to make the same trip from one town to another may have quite different passages. One may travel on a bright, sunny day and have no impediments. Another may go amid thunder and lightning and heavy rain. The third may have an accident, with serious delays and misfortune. A fourth may get lost, despite the map, and wander fruitlessly around the country for a while. Nonetheless, maps are of some value to travelers. They show that at least there is a way, and that it has been traversed before. They tell us that it is possible to make that trip because it has been made and charted. In the form of symbols—not pictures—like circles for a town, the map gives you some guidelines on how to proceed, if you also know how to read the arrows, numbers, and names you see on signs along the road. Finally, the map gives you a little bit of advance warning about possible hazards along the way, like mountains and swamps—although there is quite a large difference between a mountain range and squiggles on a piece of paper. Bearing in mind that Underhill's stages are only a map, let's look at them.

The Awakening refers to whatever it was that set one's feet on the spiritual Path; the experiences and commitments that spark Awakening are often characteristic of adolescence, though of course it may occur earlier or later. Awakening can be an extraordinary conversion or "born again" experience. For others the call may have come in the form of a calm, rather intellectual decision to try spiritual development. Some may move only gradually to a life based on deeper spiritual values than before, and not be able to pinpoint any particular moment as the time of "Awakening." On the other hand, some important spiritual figures from the past have been able to isolate specific symbol-laden revelatory moments. The Chinese Buddhist monk Mao Tzu-yuan found his call to enlightenment aroused by hearing the call of a crow at midnight. No less than the Awakening of spirit, this stage is the opening of Awareness. It is the first step on the Awareness Walk.

As discussed later Richard M. Bucke, in *Cosmic Consciousness*, tells how his especially powerful Awakening came after an evening with two friends reading the poetry of romantics such as Wordsworth, Shelley, and Whitman; as he was riding home, mulling over their ideas in a state of quiet enjoyment, he suddenly felt as though he were wrapped in flame, and a surge of immense joyousness burst upon him. The great St. Francis of Assisi received his charge from the painted lips on a crucifix in a ruined chapel, which told him to "build my church." From saints and shamans of old to contemporary mystics and "born again" Christians, reli-

gionists have known those moments, days, and years
when their world seemed to turn, and settle only when
its axis was now pointed heavenward.

But just as wakening from sleep is only the start
of day, so the awakening experience is only the com-
mencement of a spiritual life. Danger lies in investing
too much in the feelings and ideas associated with the
opening moment. That can too easily lead to fanaticism,
a roller-coaster spiritual life, and depression as the emo-
tional weather changes.

What is needed instead is what is offered in the
next stage, the Preparatory or Purgative. Ideally, if the
Awakening state is associated with adolescence, the
Preparative stage ought to follow next in young adult-
hood, if one can find time for it amidst all else that is
going on. In this stage the up-and-down tumult of the
Awakening must be steadied and stabilized. Else, one
is likely either to give up the spiritual life in cyni-
cism and despair or to continue on at an immature
level of religion that is really no more than egocentric
emotionalism.

What is called for in this stage is some spiritual prac-
tice that is steady—repeated at the same hour and for
the same length of time every day whether one "feels
like it" or not. Whether it is prayer, meditation, chant-
ing, church worship, or whatever, the important thing
is that the practice be the fruit of discipline, not of
spiritual moods and feelings. This stage is like cutting
deep and straight irrigation channels for the waters
of the spirit, not letting them merely flood or shrivel
up with the vagaries of wind and rain. The regimen
may involve a practice through which the original
awakening is recalled, even experienced again, but now

through structures that enable its energies to vitalize one's inner life and not disrupt it.

The result of spiritual practice ought to be what is called the Illuminative life; it is also the greatest fullness of Other-awareness, and is ideally most enjoyed in the later stages of young adulthood. This, for the person who essays it successfully, is the attainment of a fully "religious" life: answered prayers, a deep sense of God's presence, even visions and inner movements of divine love. For many it is enough, and they may be called to no more.

Yet there are subtle spiritual dangers attached to Illumination. People may feel they have "arrived" and tacitly shut themselves off from further growth. One may become attached to spiritual experiences as pleasures, as some are to those of the table. Because spiritual joys are especially associated with particular times and places—those of worship and meditation—there is a danger of setting up a sense of division between devotion and the rest of life, between God and the world, implying God is not yet all in all.

To purge even these remaining barriers to oneness with God in all times and places, some are called to a second Purgation—called in the classic term of St. John of the Cross the Dark Night of the Soul—in preparation for the ultimate stage, the Unitive. The Dark Night may correspond, as we have seen, with the dry years of late adulthood. Thus there may come a time, after years of great reward in Illumination or the happy practice of conventional religion, when all seems to inexplicably go dry. The ecstasies fade away and there is left only emptiness and perhaps depression. God has withdrawn Her/His presence, and all that once gave joy seems but dust and ashes. You feel chaotic and betrayed, ready to give up God and religion as delusions. It is as though you had been left in a desert at midnight without a compass.

Still, desert night air is clean and chill, and the stars, though cold and distant, blaze especially brightly. God is here in the Dark Night, but in a different way than before. Now God is less the answerer of prayers or the warm lover than a cool Presence that above all bespeaks utter purity, and infinite immensity beyond human comprehension. This God is not so much to be found in raptures, but in everything that encodes the power behind the universe.

The Dark Night is intended to cleanse us of even the subtlest sensual attachment to God or religiosity, in order to prepare us for the greatest gift of all, the Unitive state, the attainment of a deep inward oneness with God beyond times or places, beyond words or feelings. It does not need to be generated by practices, or articulated in language; if the Unitive saint follows a religious practice or speaks of God, as most do—since to separate oneself from a spiritual community would usually be an egocentric act quite at odds with Unitive selflessness—it is merely to praise the divine presence she or he knows, without needing to say so all the time.

The mystics speak of the Unitive state in a strange sort of language, as though a point has now been reached where words become frail and unreliable tools, being almost at the place where they must be abandoned altogether. We, the Unitive mystics, now know a Waylessness and a Pathlessness where one can only follow love and know God without means, we are in a Divine Dark, we are in the midst of Unborn and

Deathless Reality, neither here nor there . . . we now can see or grasp God no more than the eye can see itself or a pair of pliers grab itself . . . God is now not known in any ordinary sense . . . to know God now, one must, in Meister Eckhart's radical terms, "be rid of God, and taking the truth, break into eternity." We now know God only by unknowing God and, God-like, simply be and love. This stage can resemble the simplicity and even the despair of old age, when just to be is life enough, and all one can do for others is try to love.

Again, how do these fit in with the stages of natural life? Not necessarily at all. If we read the lives of the great saints, we find that all sorts of patterns have prevailed, from having gone through all the stages by adolescence to hardly being awakened until old age. Nonetheless, I believe that in a very large number of people, Walking the Path does, and perhaps should, correlate well with walking through the natural stages of life, in ways at which have already been hinted. Aspects of the psychology of each part of life do seem to match particularly well the requirements of a stage, and that predilection may as well be used to make the Awareness Walk that much more congenial.

To recapitulate: Infancy and childhood can be considered preparation. But the Awakening clearly goes well with the normal adolescent awakening of new emotional and physical feelings, with the teenager's yearning both for new experience and for whole-hearted commitment and romantic love, which can be directed to the divine as well as to human objects.

The Preparatory or Purgative way, then, serves as antidote to a major problem of adolescence, the way emotions and even commitments can go out of control, without balance or direction, leading to roller-coaster rides of feelings in which one extreme leads to another. The whole point of this way is to channel those feelings and bring them under the control of a spiritual training discipline.

The Illuminative way of good, happy, spiritual feelings ideally would consort with what can be called "the years of early creativity," the time of young adulthood when everything is at its height. Though they are not the same, fecundity in vocation and family life and personal maturation can be in conjunction with the conventional religious life that this state epitomizes at its best, and which is of value for most young families to have.

But life is always a matter of transitions, never staying forever—or even, in retrospect, very long—at one station. And so also with kinds of awareness along the bends of the Path. Some will be called to leave religious illumination for the sake of a deeper purgation that at the time seems like a Dark Night. On a profound inner level, the transition from young adulthood to middle age, when the children leave home and work and marriage become all too routine, can also be a Dark Night. These two Dark Nights can together be an initiation into the most wondrous potential for old age, a time of coming into the highest spiritual stage, the Unitive state.

As we have seen, life has at least three kinds of initiations: the "natural," such as birth, puberty, mothering and fathering, age, sickness, and death; the "social," such as public occasions by which religion and society endeavor to sanctify these natural initiations, such as birth and puberty rites, weddings, last rites, and funerals; and "programmed" or esoteric initiations, those into fraternities, religious orders, and spiritual paths. I think there is also a fourth kind, those by which the natural stages of life can be harmonized with the spiritual Path. Leading the reader through these initiations will be the labor of this book.

# Wake of Splendor:
## Infancy and Childhood

*Our birth is but a sleep and a forgetting:*
  *The Soul that rises with us, our life's Star,*
*Hath had elsewhere its setting,*
    *And cometh from afar:*
*Not in entire forgetfulness,*
*And not in utter nakedness,*
  *But trailing clouds of glory do we come*
    *From God, who is our home:*
  *Heaven lies about us in our infancy!*
  *Shades of the prison-house begin to close*
    *Upon the growing Boy,*
  *But he beholds the light, whence it flows,*
    *He sees it in his joy;*
*The Youth, who daily farther from the east*
  *Must travel, still is Nature's Priest,*
    *And by the vision splendid*
    *Is on his way attended;*
*At length the Man perceive it die away,*
*And fade into the light of common day.*

> —Ode: Intimations of Immortality
> *William Wordsworth*

I s this really true? Does the newborn infant really have a privileged memory of a prenatal, primordial state in which was breathed transcendent glory as naturally as is now air? Is the infant and young child in fact in close touch with the splendor that surrounds us always—and is within us always, "the imprisoned splendor"—but which we later so easily forget? Or is this only an adult fantasy?

There are accounts which support the imprisoned splendor supposition. Edward Hoffman, in *Visions of Innocence,* has collected a number of positive religious experiences of children, and following are a couple that relate to the divine in nature. "Elaine" is describing a family trip to New Brunswick when she was thirteen. Gazing out the car window, she sees a wide river opening up into "a seemingly infinite bay or ocean."

> The scene's grandeur overwhelmed me. The surprising and dramatic expanse of water reminded me of infinity, of the universe, and of God. Somehow I felt a kind of pride that I was the only one in the car who had glimpsed infinity: that great body of water, disappearing suddenly over the horizon, past the shorelines receding on either side of us. I felt a special connection to God.
>
> It was an intense and unforgettable moment, but I also experienced a sense of insignificance as a human. I was attracted to the scene by its awesome beauty and simplicity: the simplicity of eternity. . . . The seeds of my entire outlook on life were planted in me that day. . . . Remembering it still gives me a sense of life's harmony and fulfillment: how life flows naturally to its end, to

join in Infinity. The Eternal Presence is always with us.[1]

Another account is by "Michelle," who tells of an early vigil while at a Girl Scout camp in Big Bend National Park:

> I quietly awoke in the early morning, walked away from the camp, and sat on a boulder. No one else was awake yet, and the air was clear and still. I looked up and watched the flight of a big bird, probably a vulture. It glided on the air.
>
> Suddenly I felt totally transfixed. Time simply stopped. Nothing else existed. I was one with the bird and the sky as I sat on the boulder. Apparently, one of my Girl Scout friends who then saw me had to call my name repeatedly—and even became worried—in order to break the deep meditative state I was in.
>
> There were other times as a child . . . in which I felt "at one" with nature—whether it was relating to a flower, listening to the babble of a brook, gazing at a distant mountain range, or taking in the night sky.[2]

Michelle adds that, as an adult, "My main priority now is to bring this spirituality into my work in dance therapy."

However, this is not the only kind of childhood children have. What of those other childhoods in which, to say the least, the shadows of the prison-house close round very soon? What about the children of war, of abuse, of poverty and hunger? The children of Sarajevo and Rwanda? Hardly less, the children of the worst conditions in America? Alex Kotlowitz, in *There are No Children Here,* describes conditions of childhood in what he calls "the other America."[3] Kotlowitz had met Lafayette and Pharaoh Rivers in 1985, when they were ten and seven years old respectively, and living with their mother in a decaying public housing project on Chicago's West Side. The gunfire from gang wars continually punctuated their young lives. Even the police were afraid to come into this hell at the heart of one of America's great cities. LaJoe, the boys' mother, took eighty dollars a month from her already tiny welfare check to pay for burial insurance for her children. For a time Pharaoh went to some Bible classes at a local church, and tried to pray, but here is how he put the results: "I be praying but he [God] don't do nothing. Maybe there ain't no God." Nonetheless, Pharaoh found a secret place for himself where he could be alone with . . . if not God, Something. He had discovered a small patch of grass in front of a condominium a few blocks away, and it was like an island. Here he "just stayed on the lawn . . . until a security guard or janitor shooed him away, but he always left happy and satisfied. Being there for even a hour gave him a chance to catch his breath, to find the tranquility he treasured."

Indeed children have this need to be apart at times, to find out who one really is when one is not just defined by relationships with others or by roles in the world. Though they may have few words for it, children sense they also have an inner nature, known only to themselves and perhaps to God. This inward place wants to be touched and felt even if not named. It is of spirit but not always conventionally pious. Robert Coles, in his well-known *The Spiritual Life of Children,* presents a conversation between himself and Gil, a boy of Jewish background. Gil said:

> I was taking our pup for a walk and doing my thinking. That's when I'm most me! I'm not listening to anyone, and I'm not talking to anyone! I ask all these questions, and I'm not sure God hears me. Why should He? How could He ever hear everything everyone decides to say to Him? It must be hard for Him not to be nearer to us. No, I don't mean that He doesn't "live nearer." [I had asked.] I mean that He's in hiding, a little, and we're trying to find Him. We play hide-and-seek—us kids do—and once, the other day, we were playing, and I thought of the times you and I have talked, and what I say, and what you ask, and I thought: You know, Gil, you do that when you think about God and you talk about Him, and maybe He does it with us.[4]

Children, then, can have deep and perhaps unconventional thoughts—and questions—about God when they are sharing their aloneness with God, in time-outs from play and family life. And these moments are very much a part of becoming who they are.

Readers of *The Diary of Anne Frank* will recall how, living in cramped and colorless rooms and in fear of discovery by the Nazis, Anne could say:

> And in the evening, when I lie in bed and end my prayers with the words, "I thank you, God, for all that is good and dear and beautiful," I am filled with joy. Then I think about "the good" of going into hiding, of my health and with my whole being of the "dearness" of Peter, of that

which is still embryonic and impressionable and which we neither of us dare to name or touch, of that which will come sometime; love, the future, happiness and of "the beauty" which exists in the world; the world, nature, beauty and all, all that is exquisite and fine.

I don't think then of all the misery, but of the beauty that still remains. This is one of the things that Mummy and I are so entirely different about. Her counsel when one feels melancholy is: "Think of all the misery in the world and be thankful that you are not sharing in it!" My advice is: "Go outside, to the fields, enjoy nature and the sunshine, go out and try to recapture happiness in yourself and in God. Think of all the beauty that's still left in and around you and be happy!"[5]

Indeed, time and again we find that it is abused children, children surrounded by barbed wire and smoking ovens, by bombs and death, who find their secret place of refuge, a corner that is theirs, or even an inner dream or fantasy or state of consciousness, that is something other than the far too grim world around them. Aldous Huxley, in *Heaven and Hell,* spoke of the "antipodes of the mind."[6] These are those marvelous places and objects, whether evoked by inner or outer sight, that present sparkle, brilliance, color and light so much in contrast with the drab world—dark skies, workaday traffic—we face out there. The antipodes of the mind are reflected in the heavens and paradises of all religion, their jeweled gates like the heavenly Jerusalem in the Book of Revelation, or their nets of gems like the Pure Land of Buddhism. The call of the antipodes, Huxley declared, is expressed in our this-worldly fascination with such sparkles as fireworks and precious stones.

One could, of course, join certain psychoanalysts in attributing all this to far memories of the "paradise of the womb" before birth, and the shadows of the prison-house to the trauma of birth. As for the splendor of childhood, that can be set against those thinkers who have seemingly held that the child is not so much especially blessed as especially cursed. She or he is self-centered and perverse, the particular victim of original sin or original ignorance, the slave to every irrational mood and impulse, needing socialization and education to become a civilized human being.

The Chinese philosopher Xunzi (Hsun-tzu, ca. 298–238 BCE) taught that human nature is basically evil, in the sense of being totally self-centered and demanding. At birth, the child wants nothing but to be fed and held, crying until these demands are met. It is only through the example of elders and through education —great Confucian virtues that Xunzi, as a scholar in that tradition, was eager to justify—that the child changes into a being suitable for a place in adult society. Fortunately, the process is possible because of one of the infant's most eminent qualities: wanting what it does not have. Because it does not have education and adult manners, it wants them and can be taught.

In the West, St. Augustine (354–430 CE), the great theologian who more than anyone else defined the doctrine of original sin, vividly presented its baleful effects in his autobiographical *Confessions*. He tells of how, as a child only six or seven years old, he stole some pears from a neighbor's tree. He berated himself for that sin now many years later, admitting that he did not steal the fruit because he was starving or had any need for them, but out of something else altogether: a perverse desire to defy the good, to show that he could do it, to put himself above any moral law or any concern for the rights of others; in a word, pride, human self-assertion against God and the universe. Human beings, the mature Augustine taught, are invariably like that in their ordinary state, owing to Adam's sin. Until one accepts redemption in Christ, even our vaunted human freedom of will means only a choice of one sinful and selfish path over another. Until then, we are all children at heart, and in this case to be a child means to be childish.

Though it may not always be "sinful," children do have desires both to imitate the adult world and to subvert it. The same children who love to dress up in adult clothes may also enjoy literature which undercuts those who wear them for real. The insightful novelist and teacher of children's literature Alison Lurie, in *Don't Tell the Grown-Ups,* presents an intriguing case that the books children love most are those which covertly subvert the patterns and values of adulthood. Beatrix Potter's Peter Rabbit thus communicates the "concealed moral . . . that disobedience and exploration are more fun than good behavior, and not really all that dangerous, whatever Mother may say." A. A. Milne's *Winnie the Pooh* is seen as indicating a rejection of adult society in favor of "a modern version of an archetypal legend . . . the story of a peaceful animal kingdom ruled by a single benevolent human being."[7]

One critic of Lurie's hypothesis has suggested that although Lurie's "basic argument is both strong and significant," she may underestimate children's counter-needs for "security, safety, and order." [8] They may want to flout the rules and subvert the world, but not too much. They may want to go out on explorations like Christopher Robin, the child-king of the animals in *Winnie the Pooh,* but then be able to come home to mother's arms, a good meal, and a warm bed. In theological terms, they may want to know sin while keeping paradise at arm's reach.

Which is right, the child of the primal paradise or the child of original sin? My position, exemplified by Peter Rabbit and Christopher Robin, is that basically both sides are right. We do have within us an inner core of glory. This is the Pilgrim, the entity come unimaginable aeons ago from the Halls of Light, from union with the primordial One and who reflects rays from our eternal higher Self. The Pilgrim is on a journey through all the states of conditioned reality, and on this Pilgrimage has inevitably become soiled and worn from the wear and tear of the path. The seeker enters any particular life encrusted with karmic burdens that hinder the vision of the glory, both without and within, and that blinkered sight predisposes one toward selfishness based on the ignorance of the half-blind.

Yet sometimes the ignorant in their naive direct perception of the world see realities more clearly than the learned, and the blind see better through their alternative senses, highly attuned to every nuance of voice and touch, than do the sighted. In their simplicity—or their wisdom—they may have no words for such seeings, and are forced into nonverbal language: the gesture of awe, the radiant face. So it is that the child, if not always wise, sometimes peeks between the bars and shadows of the prison-house.

Many adults have such memories from childhood. The great historian of religion Mircea Eliade, in his autobiography, tells this of when he was three or four years old:

> I remember especially a summer afternoon when the whole household was sleeping. I left the room my brother and I shared, creeping so as not to make any noise, and headed toward the drawing room. I hardly knew how it looked, for we were not allowed to go in except on special occasions or when we had guests. Besides, I believe that the rest of the time the door was locked. But this time I found it open and entered, still crawling. The next moment I was transfixed with emotion. It was as if I had entered a fairy-tale palace. The roller blinds and the heavy curtains of green velvet were drawn. The room was pervaded by an eerie iridescent light. It was as though I were suddenly enclosed within a huge grape. I don't know how long I stayed there on the carpet, breathing heavily. When I came to my senses, I crept carefully across the floor, detouring around the furniture, looking greedily at the little tables and shelves on which all kinds of statuettes had been carefully placed along with the cowry shells, little crystal vials, and small silver boxes. I gazed into the large venetian mirrors in whose deep and clear waters I found myself looking very different—more grown-up, more handsome, as if ennobled by that light from another world.

I never told anyone about this discovery. Actually, I think I should not have known what to tell. Had I been able to use adult vocabulary, I might have said that I had discovered a mystery . . . I could later evoke at will that green fairyland. When I did so I would remain motionless, almost not daring to breathe, and I would rediscover that beatitude all over again; I would relive with the same intensity the moment when I had stumbled into that paradise of incomparable light. I practiced for many years this exercise of recapturing the epiphanic moment, and I would always find again the same plenitude. I would slip into it as into a fragment of time devoid of duration—without beginning and without end.

By the time he was in adolescence, however, Eliade could no longer bring himself to make that recovery:

But even though the beatitude was the same, it was now impossible to bear because it aggravated my sadness too much; by this time I knew the world to which the drawing room belonged —with the green velvet curtain, the carpet on which I had crept on hands and knees, and the matchless light—was a world forever lost.[9]

Out of an early experience like this, perhaps, came Eliade's rich mature writing of religion as based on a distinction of the sacred and the profane: on a sense that reality is not homogeneous, but within the wearisome, ordinary, "profane" world are outcroppings of sacred space and time, the space of the "hierophany" or revelation of the divine, and of temples and pilgrimage sites; the sacred time of rite and festival. The sacred in all cases ultimately refers back to the *illud tempus* of the beginning, when God or the gods made the world, when time was "strong" and in a real sense eternal—the time of sunrise origins, of when most of reality had not yet solidified, of when the universe was still mostly light, and crystalline space, and the powers of imagination of the first sons of God.

I recall an experience, akin to Eliade's, that when I was perhaps five or six years old, I liked to sit under a peony bush in the back of our yard, and there I would have a fantasy—if indeed it was a fantasy—that I was not really living as the son of my family in a small city in Illinois. Instead, I was floating through space, surrounded by stars and planets such as I had seen in my astronomy books, and my life as a small boy was only a story I was telling myself. My childish form, my parents, the town amid the flat cornfields of central Illinois, perhaps even the whole planet Earth, were but figments of my imagination.

Children may also have memories of invisible friends, or may be in touch with playmates from another realm of being, suggesting other dimensions of life and of reality than the ordinary. Magical sorts of practices, such as carrying about a "good luck" amulet or not stepping on cracks, may have significance for a child. No doubt there are psychological explanations for many of these things, and it is not necessary to take any of them too seriously as insights into the absolute nature of reality. But it is also important to recall that any explanation of a subjective experience—psychological, religious, metaphysical—is simply a kind of language designed to interpret the experience by placing it in the context of other situations in which the same language is used, and therefore to place it into an interpretive framework that may or may not be the only possible one for the original experience. One might interpret a vision, or a childhood experience like Eliade's or mine, as only a psychological projection or state of consciousness, or—as certain Buddhists consider mind-formed images of cosmic Buddhas or of blissfully altered states of mind—as no more absolutely real in themselves than anything else, but they might nonetheless feel that they are useful stepping-stones on the path to ultimate enlightenment.

Consider the effects of socialization on children's religion—or perhaps one should say on how these inchoate but brilliant perceptions of sin and glory are made into religion. For children are not living in isolation from society during their experiences, although time-outs from work and play may be important to their development. We do not live apart from society —like Mowgli the Jungle boy—religiously or in any other way. We are completed and fulfilled by the connections we have with others, from family to nation. And, in my view, the difference between spiritual experiences "in the raw" and religion is that religion also is not practiced in isolation; it is a shared perception of the nature of transcendent realities held by two or more people together.

Religious societies can range from a tiny sect or cult to a great faith embracing half the world—but in either case a shared religion is a profoundly different kind of experience from one that is totally private and personal. The shared religion is talked about by people who understand and use the same language; it is confirmed by people sharing and reporting experiences that seem to come out of, or are interpreted as confirming, the same transcendental reality. It is also language-driven; any religion provides a vocabulary by which spiritual experiences are interpreted and, in the nature of things, by which they are also shaped.

A person in one religious community, having an experience of brilliant light, might say, "I had a vision of God," and may well associate personality, even voices, with the vision. A person in another community might call such an experience Nirvana and note that it was silent and impersonal. A skeptic might attribute a vision to regression to infantile "oceanic" consciousness, or a drug flashback. Naming the experience evaluates it and places it in the context of the person's social life.

In any case, the language a child uses—or hears used—to describe a religious experience makes the experience a confirmation of the religious world of one's parents, aunts and uncles, and community—unless, instead, it legitimates rebellion against them. And the words connected to one experience may facilitate having additional experiences that are part of the same religious system. Describing an experience enhances and sharpens it, like focusing an image on a screen. On the other hand, as we have seen, some childhood religious experiences may be preserved as private, not spoken of to others until much later, like Eliade's or my own—and their meaning may sometimes be ambiguous in terms of conventional religion. Yet even so the child will need to use some form of language to remember it and tell it to her- or himself, if to no one else.

The fact that we do not live in isolation helps make spiritual experience into religion in another way, too. As Freudians have consistently reminded us, people in a culture—and above all parents—serve as models for the child's religious world. It is natural that she or he would first think of gods and goddesses as Father and Mother writ large, and perhaps conflate vague memories of the "paradise of the womb" with the deep moments of mystical experience.

In all sorts of ways, then, from unconsciously imposed models of the divine to family faith to formal religious instruction in church, temple, or school, meaning-systems appear to guide, interpret, and possibly in some cases inhibit the heaven that surrounds the child in infancy. Whether the many words that religions use, the many pictures and statues, organ chords and cathedral spires, ultimately enhance innocent primal faith or are beginning shadows of the prison-house, one will have to decide for oneself. Certainly, with no words at all, most experiences would be meaningless to the word-based human mind; they could hardly be talked about, even to oneself. But need they be framed or talked about in only one language?

We can't, however, live without some socialization, some buying into the social construction of reality around us, including the religious. This is not only necessary if we are to survive and prosper in the environment, it is also necessary to our own human and spiritual maturation. For we humans really are spun into a web of interrelationships. All nature as well as all human society is interconnected; this is not only a bind, it is also the occasion for the exercise of the supreme virtue in most religions—that of love or compassion. Apart from the occasional holy hermit who may practice compassion almost entirely in the context of nature—the plants and animals who are also worthy objects of our compassion—love will be expressed in some way through the human community.

Here in community the growing child learns mutual dependence, learns that there are structures within which life is properly lived, learns the many meanings of love. Some of the lessons seem to be contradictory. We learn as children that there must be some structure in the social order and that some people have the authority that goes with it: the teacher in the classroom, the parent protecting and directing the child at home, the policeman on the street upholding the laws of the state. Yet we also learn that love must sometimes break through the social structures, and that duty can call past them. In the same way, we can accept the religious structures given us, yet be confused by instances when they do not seem to fit—when the innocent suffer, the unjust do not receive their comeuppance, when spirituality runs dry and prayers go unanswered.

Such times are understandably confusing to a child (as they may be to adults, too), and the child may thus take one of several paths. For example, one path may be to repress doubts because of the seeming greater value of conformity, or because strong positive experiences associated with the religion, subjective or social, so outweigh the negative as to overwhelm them and assure the child that it all must nonetheless be true. Others will go into rebellion, as have countless children who have removed religious garb out of sight of their parents, or stopped attending services as soon as they left home. More, perhaps, will hold both the believing and the doubting sides in tension. Consciously or unconsciously, they are open to a little bit of skepticism and a little bit of faith, letting each temper the other. For them the potent inner inchoate early childhood experiences, and the positive structures of religion, must push against all the disconfirming observations offered by the world. All this may be laid down like a depth charge somewhere along the childhood road, waiting to go off before the end of life. So all this is another outer contour of childhood religion: occasional experiences of splendor, structures of thought and life being put into place that provide images for religion while also channeling it; potential for deep-level tension between the religious private-personal world and outer realities.

But what about the esoteric meaning of childhood religion? As a new life commences, the Pilgrim is negotiating a working agreement between three forces: the inner self irradiated by one's eternal higher Self or Monad; the burden of karmic debts and propensities brought over from before; and the circumstances (karmically-prepared, but new to this entity) of the present life. The confusions of childhood are reduced finally to the conflicts inherent in this negotiating process. For children know that they are not just a simple, one-dimensional self. Whether they have words for it or not, they know that they have, first, an inner identity—who I am when I'm alone, thinking quietly, dreaming—the self that Pharaoh contacted in his tranquil patch of grass, or that Eliade found in the green room.

Second, there is who I am when I'm angry or afraid. Sometimes I may not even entirely know why I'm angry or afraid, or why there are things in this world with which my inner nature seems to collide. On this level, there is also who I am when I'm playing—especially when alone, playing out stories that come from I know not where. This is the karma-woven level of self trying to make its peace with a new physical vesture and a new world.

Finally, there is who I am when I'm adapting to the ways of this world, when I line up with the other nascent children of this new world to go into class or visit the zoo, when I am a good child at home, when I pray in like manner to everyone else at church or temple.

But getting these three selves together is not easy. One adapts, but sometimes the inexplicable fear and anger and the rest of the karmic caravans dragged past the customs-posts of this world kick and buck impetuously, and it is all one can do to keep them under wraps. And "something else" may be demanding radiant contemplation, and does not seem to understand the laborious necessities of life on this particular planet. The eyes of a child may appear to look steadily at the world, but in their depths something seems to be flitting back and forth anxiously, as though it were an older bundle of restless energy trapped in a new body; and behind this, even deeper, shines through those same eyes the clear light of something born free and never fallen wholly into matter.

Compromises there will be. The eternal Pilgrim is largely forgotten for the sake of this world; the old self repressed to make life go smoothly here, or else given free reign to create a social rebel, with or without a cause. (Sometimes one may rebel for a very good cause.) Adjustments can vary. Wise parents, guardians, and

teachers can guide young wards toward a balanced res-
olution: maintaining individuality for one's unique
karmic and genetic heritage without destructive rebel-
lion; upholding positive values of the culture without
sterile conformity; and, more subtly, letting the Pilgrim
shine in, around, and through the forms of everyday
life—letting the Pilgrim be seen, as it were, from time
to time in the mirror. For the ultimate goal to every life
is to know the Pilgrim, to let it unite completely with
its Monad or higher Self, and to make the rest of life
so transparent that it can see and know itself—for each
day to be a reflecting glass of the eternal within.

So let parents, guardians, and teachers see that chil-
dren not only maintain the balance between heritage
and society, but also have time out just to know and be
themselves. Let them play alone or with invisible com-
panions, let them just sit and think and dream, let them
search far memories, let them look in the mirror for the
light behind the eyes, let them begin to meditate if only
briefly.

And all this is only a prelude to the Awakening for
those who will consciously, or even semi-consciously,
take up Walking the Path in this lifetime.

## Questing and Nesting:
### Adolescence and Young Adulthood

N ow comes the Pilgrim to puberty and adolescence. Big questions push themselves forward, like this one: How is life defined?

One way to look at it is this. A human life is a series of points of dynamic and creative encounters between Self and outer world. Neither comes to the meeting bare or unprepared. I—the Self—come with all that I have ever been, for as the poet said, "I am a part of all that I have met." The encounter is creative. We partly discover the world, we partly make it in the act of thinking we are discovering it. The world as we see it is but the last wave crashing upon the shores of visibility, blown by the endless winds of karma. For those karmic gales are made out of the visions, choices, fears, and dreams of the countless beings on all the planes of Earth, and on all the other worlds whose sunrises they have seen in aeons before the oldest memories of today. Each conscious entity is a grain of sand battered by that endless sea, a face in a measureless hall of mirrors; a touch anywhere ripples and reflects faster than light through the whole. Your consciousness and mine are but sand-soft knots of light swiftly tied and untied by those incoming mazes of waves from the boundless sea. Yet we can determine how, in our time, in the day that is given to us, we face the waves. Even how we see them. Do we ride their crests and see their finer droplets rainbow and golden in the sun? Or are we crushed and sucked into their dark undertows?

In adolescence and youth this issue faces the Pilgrim with particular force in the context of each lifetime. For now is the time when the question of one's adult identity is pressing in hard, and its resolution cannot long be put off. At the same time, the fresh and powerful energies surging through the adolescent—emotional, sexual, idealistic; the craving for experience, for authority and truth, for independence—make for a confused and confusing template for that new life.

The teenager and young adult is far from completely disconnected from childhood, and from the family within which the earlier life was nestled. Incredibly powerful magnetic forces of attraction or repulsion— or both at once—may play between family and adolescent. No matter how well childhood was coordinated, the ship of one's life is bound to encounter heavy seas as puberty arrives, and powerful new energies reach gale force. It is a stormy passage through which to set a life course, yet somehow it must be done. Compass coordinates for the journey are the four basic drives that can be identified in adolescence: new emotional experience, the desire for individuation, the need for peer acceptance, and a yearning for a clear-cut worldview and values to go with it.

First, consider new emotional experiences: Most of us can probably remember the first real surge of sexual feeling we had in puberty, and the first time we felt a powerful attraction connected with those feelings for another person. We may have thought, as have millions of teenagers, that no one else in human history could ever have been so powerfully in love; that it was, as for Romeo and Juliet, something to die for. We have sexual drives and the emotions to go with them; nature wants us to bond with another of our species on all sorts of levels. Such feelings can indeed lead to terrible distress, or even thoughts of suicide, as well as unimaginable ecstasy when the right person calls and there is that perfect afternoon on the beach or just hanging out together. Life can indeed be an emotional roller coaster.

That is no less true when the potent new emotions are attached to apparently nonsexual objects as well. The fervent adolescent commitment may be to social or political idealism, or to the field of honor. For adolescence is also the age of the warrior, from the medieval knight to those who in our own century, sometimes with great heroism and self-sacrifice, fought on all sides of wars from Flanders Fields to the steamy islands of the South Pacific. Sometimes two varieties of commitments, the spiritual and the temporal, are but two sides of the same thing. Thus, adolescence is for some a golden age of religious awakening, conversion and commitment. Then—as for innumerable mystics through the ages—God may be loved as passionately as ever was any earthly beloved. You can see that, correlating the basic cycles of normal human life and the spiritual Path, adolescence fits in with the Awakening stage. The psychology is right.

With any Awakening there is always danger. A great peril is that of absolutizing one's first powerful adolescent emotional experiences, whether romantic or religious. Very understandably, one may think, "This is so strong there can't be anything more. The person I love so fervently, as Romeo loved Juliet, must be the only person I could ever so love; or, the truth about God and salvation I have experienced here must be as great as Paul's on the Damascus road, and must reveal absolute and final truth." Yet as we know, all too often the most passionate and tender teenage love may hit the divorce courts a few years later, and the most glorious spiritual ecstasies go sour, either in the bitter fanaticism of clinging to that whose time is past, or in an ice age of mocking doubt.

Two things are wrong with this primal absolutism as regards spirituality. First, a strong emotion is not the same thing as a profound spiritual insight or a revelation of final truth. It is just an emotion, which can be a manifestation of certain glands and may be attached to all sorts of symbols and ideas. Religious or mystical feelings do rightly tell us there is more to life than the ordinary. But these feelings are like opening the door just a crack, and are not the same as making oneself at home in the whole house on the other side. Remember that most great spiritual masters tell us that the highest spiritual experiences are very soft, subtle, calm, and clear, not wild and stormy.

That leads to the second problem, which is that emotions fluctuate. Except in the case of seriously disturbed persons, who may be chronically depressed or manic, any powerful emotion is bound to give way to a contrasting feeling in time. Most of us have had the experience of an intense feeling, whether of joy or sorrow, being replaced sooner or later by a sort of emotional numbness. If one is greatly enraptured, whether through some human joy such as falling in love or through a rich religious experience of conversion or mystical union, the time will come when that feeling is no longer so strongly felt. It is the same with feelings of deep grief. The sentiment may linger in the form of recurrent bubbles of feeling, or of a deep but calm underground stream in one's life, but the high winds and preternatural lights are gone.

Some people find that very distressing, and may even fall into feelings of guilt: "I must not really have loved that person after all, or else I would still feel passionate joy or grief," or "I must have committed some great sin, or I must not have really believed in God, or God would not have withdrawn from me." But that attitude is very much off base, and can lead to much unnecessary suffering. Love and divine grace are not measured by intensity of emotional feeling, but by a quiet and steady living in the glow of the other's life, whether the other is human (and in that event, whether physically present or departed) or divine.

All these are matters adolescents have to learn about and deal with. However, that is especially a problem because the adolescent, even more than most of the rest of us, is acutely self-conscious and self-aware. Her or his feelings are likely to be taken as absolute, ultimate reality; or, to put it another way, they are a weather-system from which there seems no escape. One must take them as is, be whatever they are at the time: angry, fearful, passionate, depressed, jealous, whatever. Only little by little does the adolescent gain the capacity to observe intense feelings from a center of consciousness within, yet also be able to stand apart from moods and feelings. Yet the adolescent knows that somehow she or he has to become a person, not just a kaleidoscope of alternating feelings. This is the drive which, to use the Jungian term, is called individuation. Nothing is harder, but nothing is more important.

Shakespeare has given us unforgettable tragic figures based on the profound psychological tensions and temptations humans experience in each of the major periods of adult life: *Romeo and Juliet* and *Hamlet* for youth and awakening, *Othello* for the creative Illuminative years of early adulthood, and *King Lear* for middle age and the Dark Night of the Soul. Because these plays are tragedies, they obviously represent the unsuccessful transiting of the years; we can learn from them the temptations and opportunities for mischance specific to each. We will end, however, with the figure of Prospero in *The Tempest,* who represents old age and opportunity for successfully approaching the Unitive state.

First, consider *Romeo and Juliet* and *Hamlet*. The two plays are both about adolescence, but the picture of that stage of life is far from the same. The "star-cross'd lovers" of Verona may be early adolescents, the Prince of Denmark late, but far more important is the youthful mood each presents: Romeo and his beloved show the intensity, the commitment, and the idealization of the Awakening; Hamlet the uncertainty, the powerful conflicting emotions only half-understood, the tension between family and freedom, between study and life—those of a hypersensitive college-age youth like himself.

Esoterically, the new problem for these years is that of readjusting the three selves of childhood in light of the new physical and emotive self one now is. Who one is alone, who one is angry and afraid, who one is with others and stepping out in the world, clearly have quite different meanings when drenched with sexuality, and when the lights of conversion and questioning play over them. The Pilgrim, the karmic self, and the social self will need to go back to school and undertake painful readjustment. To get them right may require balance-of-power maneuvers worthy of the most astute diplomat; unfortunately they must be made by an inexperienced youth with hormones raging. Yet, with help, some succeed.

Not all. The new life is first of all overwhelmingly confusing. One cannot go back to an old world of supposedly innocent childhood, yet one knows not how to proceed forward either. Romeo, toward the beginning of his play, describes well the chaos of feeling that adolescent love, and above all frustrated love, produces:

Why, then, O brawling love! O loving hate!
O any thing, of nothing first create!
O heavy lightness! serious vanity!
Mis-shapen chaos of well-seeming forms!
Feather of lead, bright smoke, cold fire, sick health!
Still-waking sleep, that is not what it is!
This love feel I, that feel no love in this.
Dost thou not laugh?

Then out of the chaos can come a sense of direction as desperate as it is powerful, strong from beating against the barriers of an unfeeling world, and withal tender from the love and pity surging within in ways the world, it thinks, can barely guess. A little later, seeing Juliet above in a window, her lover expresses the passionate idealism and commitment of youth at its most intense, commitment that would lead to double deaths:

> But, soft! what light through yonder window
>     breaks?
> It is the east, and Juliet is the sun.
> Arise, fair sun, and kill the envious moon,
> Who is already sick and pale with grief,
> That thou her maid art far more fair than she:
> Be not her maid, since she is envious;
> Her vestal livery is but sick and green
> And none but fools do wear it; cast it off,
> It is my lady, O, it is my love!

Hamlet is another stage of adolescence. A student, he is interested in ideas. Like many adolescent intellectuals, he takes refuge in books and ideas out of terror of the feelings churning within him, seeking outlets but allowed none by his fears and the social pressures that he is unable to handle; at the same time, he is clumsy with anything but the dry leaves of words, angry at them, yet unable to do anything else but think. The Pilgrim is eclipsed by the karmic self, and then is trapped in eddying pools unable to flow. Emotions rise within the heir of Denmark far stronger than the thirst for knowledge. "What do you read, my lord?" asks Polonius to the young prince in his library. "Words, words, words," the latter replies, and then goes into a spate of wordy madness mocking the pomposities of scholarly and literary scribes. He wants real life, whatever that is exactly; and moreover, he is consumed with emotion about his family. Hamlet is convinced that his uncle, now seated on the throne and married to his mother, murdered his father. So it was at least that his father's ghost told him, and after giving his son that dreadful news, said, "Adieu, adieu! Hamlet, remember me"; that memory was at least one rising of the dam that held back the emotional flow. To that admonition of his father's ghost the prince replied, wanting security even if it was in the firmness of his hatreds,

> O all you host of heaven! O earth! what else?
> And shall I couple hell? O, fie! Hold, hold,
> > my heart;
> And you, my sinews, grow not instant old. But
> > bear me stiffly up.
> Remember thee!
> Ay, thou poor ghost, while memory holds a seat
> In this distracted globe. Remember thee!
> Yea from the table of my memory
> I'll wipe away all trivial fond records,
> All saws of books, all forms, all pressures past,
> That youth and observation copied there . . .
> . . . yes, by heaven!
> O most pernicious woman!
> O villain, villain, smiling, damned villain!
> My tables,—meet it is I set it down,
> That one may smile, and smile,
> > and be a villain.

Let these lines stand for the ways in which family matters and complex emotions, even if not as extreme as the circumstances which confronted Hamlet's unsteady disposition, can run at cross purposes to the peaceful flow of education and maturation for teenagers. Note that even the bizarre and tumultuous situation of meeting his father's ghost on a gloomy night has not completely overridden Hamlet's habits as a student; though he says that the appalling revelation will wipe away "all saws of books," he still wants to set down in his "tables" the bottom-line lesson he learned, like any student taking notes.

As to what to do next, however, Hamlet is typically undecided. In the famous soliloquy he says:

> To be, or not to be: that is the question;
> Whether 'tis nobler in the mind to suffer
> The slings and arrows of outrageous fortune,
> Or to take arms against a sea of troubles,
> And by opposing end them? To die: to sleep;
> No more; and by a sleep to say we end
> The heart-ache and the thousand natural shocks
> That flesh is heir to, 'tis a consummation
> Devoutly to be wish'd.
> To sleep: Perchance to dream: ay, there's the rub . . .

Torn thus between the ideal of action and withdrawal, even through the means of suicide, then uncertain as to what death would bring, Hamlet shows his real adversary is a sea of words and ideas. Suicide would not release him, no more than it releases anyone from karma. He has enough learning to convince him how little he really knows, above all about how to act. Adolescents really know very little; sometimes they realize this, sometimes they cover over their doubts with braggadocio.

The same blockage obtains in Hamlet's relationship with Ophelia, to whom he is clearly deeply attracted in his confused way. Often adults, seeing only golden bodies of youth, or perhaps projecting their own fantasies on them, imagine them in some intuitive way already adept in the erotic arts. Not so; they are not so easily mastered. The equipment may be there, but a fine palette does not make a Picasso. Hamlet has far to go in expression, and much stands in the way of skilled forward motion with voice or hand. Like many persons who live in the mind, he is out of touch with emotions, especially those involved in relationships with others, and above all with the physical expression of heart and soul. In his encounters with Ophelia he has nothing to say in words, however many he has to express his own inner agonies. Only awkward physical gestures come to him. Here is how Ophelia herself describes it:

> He took me by the wrist and held my hand;
> Then goes he to the length of all his arm;
> And, with his other hand thus o'er his brow,
> He falls to such perusal of my face
> As he would draw it. Long stay'd he so;
> At last, a little shaking of mine arm
> And thrice his head thus waving up and down,
> He raised a sigh so piteous and profound
> As it did seem to shatter all his bulk
> And end his being: that done, he lets me go;
> And, with his head over his shoulder turn'd
> He seem'd to find his way without his eyes;
> For out o'doors he went without their helps,
> And, to the last, bended their light on me.

All of us bend the lights of our eyes upon some-thing, and the world is reflected in the eyes and our eyes in the world as we see it. For the world is also a mirror, lit by the lights within the face. In a deep sense, we see what we put there. Those whose inward-ness is full of joy and beauty see a world bursting with beauty and packed with much to make one joyous. Those who are full of anger see the world as rent with anger and occasions of anger; those full of love, as overflowing with love and lovable objects.

But we also seek to change the lay of the world, especially as adolescents and young adults, and to some extent we succeed. How? By the power of Will, if it is bright and pure enough, and is not stifled like Hamlet's.

Yet Will needs guideposts. What kind? What would be strong enough to contain and direct the oft-rebellious passions of youth? Consider myth. Myths are very important to adolescents. Even the most rebellious and unpleasant of young people—gang members, loners, hackers and nerds—are acting out of some dream or vision or ideal self in the mind. They want to be that actor in some story they are telling themselves, in their own myth. For myths offer patterns for that all-important transition between inner feelings and outer action —that at which Hamlet failed so miserably, and which all adolescents want somehow to carry off well. Abstract words are not enough; what tells us best how to act is stories—stories one can identify with on one end, and which lead to transcendent and inevitable levels of success on the other. Myths and other forms of popular entertainment do this. That is why adolescents like movies, which almost always have a mythical motif somewhere in the background. Even video games are myths, like those of the heroine's or hero's trials and triumphs. The Shakespearean stories may be myths of failure, but there are also myths of success.

We need to understand that in spiritual writing the word myth does not mean what it usually means today to the ordinary person, simply a story that is not true. Rather, myth means a narrative that, whether it is true in the literal factual sense or not, expresses the truths of inner psychological and spiritual reality in story form.

Myths may be divided into two types. The creation myth tells the story of how the world came into being. It is important because you can always assume that if you know fully and deeply where something came from, you know important things about its true nature. This is the myth of the Pilgrim and the roots of the quest, and it must be rediscovered in adolescence. Toward the end of a creation myth, however, there is likely to be an episode, like the expelling of Adam and Eve from the Garden of Eden in Genesis, which indicates that something has gone wrong, and the right relations that originally existed between the creation and its source have been lost. Here is where the hero (or heroine) and the hero-myth comes in. The hero genre has great appeal for teenagers.

The hero or heroine, on an individual basis, restores right relations between the one and the other. Sometimes this may be a conventional military hero, like Rama, or an explorer like Ulysses, whose exploits may be read allegorically as types of the ultimate victory. In such models or founders of the great religions as Krishna, the Buddha, or Jesus, however, we have warriors of the spirit who through love, meditation, and suffering on a heroic scale have actually overcome the gap and, as pioneers of salvation, have opened a gate through which others can proceed whither they went.

Then there are the myths of love—of Romeo and Juliet, Psyche and Cupid, Tristan and Isolde, Snow

White and the Prince. These are myths, often painful, of the burgeoning of Other-awareness on the Awareness Walk in its most acute form, an awareness that somewhere—not necessarily in every lifetime—must be met and mastered and understood by all, when the time is right.

George Russell, the remarkable Irish theosophical visionary, mystic, and social reformer who wrote under the name Æ,[1] penned a few poems of theosophical flavor mythically reflecting creation, hero, and love. A mystical theosophical vision of creation as coming from a source outside of time and close to pure thought is suggested by this example:

### Ancient

The sky is cold as pearl
Over a milk-white land,
The snow seems older than Time
Though it fell through a dreaming and
Will vanish itself as a dream
At the dimmest touch of a hand.

Out of a timeless world
Shadows fall upon Time,
From a beauty older than earth
A ladder the soul may climb,
I climb by the phantom stair
To a whiteness older than Time.

In every pair of young lovers the archetype of Pilgrims descending from the Halls of timeless light into time is reproduced, though the eternal remains buried in the heart of all those on pilgrimage, and may be forgotten by them in a personal equivalent of what is

QUESTING AND NESTING   79

meant by the Fall. When it is retained, all barriers to the glory of the Beginning and the End are overcome. In these poems, though, the glory is lost, as so often, to be recovered, we hope, before the end.

### The Eternal Lovers

Whirled on their starry Odyssey
From heaven to earth, in this deep glade
The eternal lovers hold their court
Within the heart of man and maid.

That darkness throbs with hidden fire:
The pulse beats fast: the heavens call:
Earth is transfigured, and the twain
Breathe as they did before the Fall.

When King and Queen feast in the heart
They squander all the gold of years
To make their banquet gay, then leave
A ruined heart, a house of tears.

And again:

### The Lost Others

You set your heart on Nancy.
You won your fancy, lad.
But love had never taught you
What other names she had,
Or what gay Naiad lent her grace,
What shining Oread.

You did not know what beauty
thronged in that light disguise:
What eyes gazed out of Faery,
What Sibyl from the Wise,

What burning miracle her soul
Was in its native skies.

You won your pretty Nancy;
But she was all you had.
The starry women vanished.
A lonely lass and lad
Mutely upon each other gaze
Nor know why they are sad.

The importance of myth to adolescents is for the
sake of identification with an ideal self-image, and for
the action of a story that can lead them to understand
what is happening to them. In this time of self-discov-
ery, they above all want to know who they are at their
highest and greatest; to know that like those beings in
Æ's poems, they are kings and queens, and beings of
light, though currently in the midst of grime. This a
mythic narrative can give them, in simple and clear and
action-laden terms.

In search of this meaning, we may first be led to
read the old Greek myths, or a living national myth
cycle, such as the Kojiki or national epic of Japan; or
the Hebrew scriptures of Judaism and Christianity,
which tell the story of Israel's tribes and their relation-
ships with God from the days of Abraham and Moses,
from the covenant and the Red Sea crossing to the end
of the ancient kingdom. But we need to realize, too,
that myths begin with a single scene, a snapshot or
fragment, like our own memories and dreams. Myth
"in the raw," so to speak, is not the long epic probably
constructed at a later stage out of single mythic scenes.
These primordial scenes are, like key memories, ulti-
mately timeless and still, caught in those immortalized

in statuary: Perseus holding up the severed head of Medusa, Krishna in his eternal play with the milkmaids across the immortal fields of the heavenly Vrindaban, Jesus on the cross frozen into a thousand crucifixes. These mythic snapshots serve our purpose, for what we really want in identifying with myth is to catch hold of a starting point that is itself timeless. From there we can write our own story.

Imagine for example, in our own society, a teenage girl and boy both reading the New Testament. She has heard of other persons like her reading of the luminous figure of Jesus as he appears there, and is taken with his story, in a way that makes him seem alive now, indeed standing beside her, as her best and most forever friend. She has heard of people being "born again" as they accept this Christ. She feels a surge of power and she responds to the utter majesty of this tale. She knows her own unworthiness, the many sins that lie at her door, as she looks on Jesus. As the boy reads, he sees Jesus growing and growing as a figure of power, healing the sick, giving wise teaching, utterly unafraid in the presence of his enemies, finally giving up his life, yet unconquered by death. He knows that he belongs to Jesus, and in a brief tearful prayer, accepts him and vows to follow him as though he were the thirteenth disciple. But the manner in which they both will respond to Jesus is, so to speak, to write another chapter to the Acts of the Apostles, as they become apostles themselves through their lives. Though they may have many models in scripture and the lives of more recent Christians, their lives of faith will also be uniquely their own paths; the teenagers will both write their own chapters of Acts themselves.

To break out of the story into the immediacy of the mythic moment is to experience freedom. But the pressures are powerful to stay inside the bounds of the story, which is what gives force to conversion experiences like the ones above. We must conform ourselves to the myth, and then break out of it enough to live in its light here and now. This is not an easy process to sort out. How does one do so? By the power of Will, if it is bright and pure enough.

What can Will do? Do we really change external reality, or only our seeing of it? Who can say? Does the rising sun change land and sea, or only cast a shower of gold, and then all the rainbow colors, over them? Do rock and wave change the sun by receiving its radiance and making it visible? Suffice it to say that no system in this universe is solitary, standing apart from all the rest in mood or might; all are made by the whole and manifest that whole in every detail. And what we know, how we know, is determined by the brightness and purity of mind. There is much to see that can only be seen when, as Blake said, the doors of perception are cleansed; there may be much further that can only come into being as it is perceived by cleansed eyes, and when behind them there is a mind whose eye is single. Let there be among the young those with eyes to see a better world, and by their saying, "Let there be light," may that world form into being, if only as a sphere around each of them!

And what will be the landscape of that better world, with its slow rivers and shining mountains? First, there will be love, personal and in its universal aspect, manifested as equality and respect for all. Second, vocation. Let there be a sense that life is not just something you fall into, in which what you do is done through chance or the course of least resistance, but that everyone has on some level a unique calling; something—whether in paid work or in a volunteer vocation or within the family or in some other way—that is uniquely yours to do. If you do not do it, it will not be done for all eternity, so it is desperately important that this task is found and is done by you. Finally, God. God will be seen, not quite with physical eyes, but as a Light, a Presence, that makes all things more clear, more distinct and real, just as they are—yet draws them all together, united by those cords of light.

These three themes will appeal to youth at their highest and most idealistic, because these are times when one is supremely finding what love and the potent emotions behind it mean, when one is discovering anew one's individuality—who one is when one is alone—and when one also must deal with the task of what to do with a life that still lies ahead. And it is also a time when God—whatever is meant by God—can be a most important issue. Yet life is also there to be lived. For youth is a time to enjoy the world in all its richness and diversity—to throw coins in the Trevi fountain in Rome, as well as pray in baroque churches, to hike the Sierras and talk all night in student flats, to explore and know solitude and the counterworld of dreams.

But without clear sight all this will go sour, and tentacles will reach out of the morass to hold you to one thing or another in the moving world, and then as time moves on you will be stretched thin to the breaking point. For nothing in life is worth anything unless it can be let go of. Then it becomes memory and is forever.

Seeing everything as crystalline and distinct should be done in time as well as in space. A particular power of youth is that time is at its most expansive. Time may actually seem unreal, even as death, time's sharpest reminder of its reality, seems unreal. This makes accessible to youth the timeless moment of myth. At the height of one's physical force it is hard to seriously believe one will die. This is an untruth, and the youth knows it, but death is no inner ticking clock and it does not seem a real presence. The relative absence of time and death must be received in youth as a gift; but like all gifts it should not be clung to past its own time.

The other side to this is that young people *are* time. For they are oriented to the future, to its plans and dreams, to its deferred rewards. Timeless as adolescence sometimes seems, then, youth must get ready for the future. That is why there is the yearning for belief and commitment, and the experience of romantic love and marriage. And—remember the poems of Æ—human romantic love and marriage are not just *human* love and marriage, but are also emblems and means toward the ultimate quest. Sometimes, these relationships may exist because they establish important karmic relationships carried over out of space and time. But they are to be dealt with in this life, possibly even now to be finished.

But that is only looking at relationships on the level of time in which karma operates. On the still deeper level of the timeless Monad (as Theosophy might call it) of each of us, romantic love is participation in the eternal unfallen level of reality. It is a return to the halls of light where all are kings and queens, where all bear visibly the light of eternity, where the two can again become one, where all that was lost is found.

This is the fullest potential of the adolescent Awakening. It is therefore no less divine than any other stage of life.

# The Sun in Strength:
## The Years of Early Creativity

Here is a paradox: The transition from youth to adulthood is characteristically one of a radical inward shift from receiving to giving, from being someone else's responsibility to exercising responsibility, even as one also has certain newfound kinds of freedom. One is no longer a guest at the banquet of life, but becomes a host. The host has freedom to select the menu, within limits of availability, but how many obligations go with that honorable office!

The years now under consideration, the twenties and thirties, are busy and demanding. The shift in role from guest to host does not occur overnight; often throughout these years you might seem to be alternating from one to the other. In any case, school, work, romance, parenting, and plain enjoyment of life when your full energies are available in its service take up most of your time and thought. It is a time of outflowing and inflowing. The Path may well be half forgotten, even by those who were once aware of it, at a time when "just living" takes up so much of life. To be sure, you can be following the Path even when it is forgotten. But there is more to it than that. When the sun is in strength, it may be assumed that the living of such a life *is* the path—that one's spirituality is to work, to love, to parent, to play.

In this too lies a grand and deep truth. The physical, material side of life *is* of great importance to your pilgrimage in these years. The Pilgrim, riding the sun-carriage now being pulled by vigorous chargers into the city of material wonders and fleshly delights, is alert and alive to every joy seen out the windows. The Pilgrim comes into her or his realm striving to perceive and comprehend them all, disdaining none provided they are truly of matter and flesh.

But life is on many levels and harbors many illusions as well as many joys. Not all that glitters is gold, not all that seems to wear garments of flesh and matter is really such, but may be coarse and low spirits in disguise. As with all spirits, their true abode is not in matter; they are instead intruders from unwholesome realms into the caverns of our minds. From there they can be expelled, but they do not go easily and are the great enemies of the young adult.

Remember that what is truly bodily delight is what is natural to the body in its simple, straightforward, nonverbal character; what is added on by fevered imagination and fantasy is from the brain, not the flesh, and so is of a lower spiritual (actually, lower astral) origin. The body itself wants only plain, wholesome, natural food and drink; excessive and exquisite substances catering to pampered tastes, or which supposedly affirm one's prosperity or lifestyle, or which answer to craving for intoxication or drug-dreams, honor not the body but are fantasies concocted on the low level from which ordinary dreams and fantasies come, and they distort our honest body/spirit nature as truly as does excessive and unhealthy asceticism. The body itself needs only the natural expression of sexuality in marriage; other materializations of it stem not from bodily needs originally, but from sexual fantasies built up in the brain, and are often stimulated by unreal notions of sexual attractiveness derived from magazines and movies more than from real people.

Again, life is on many levels. We have mentioned three selves: the Pilgrim, the karmic self, the social self. These may be further broken down into others. The theosophical tradition relates that we have several interpenetrating "bodies"—the physical, the "astral" or feeling and desire-laden, the mental, the intuitive, and the spiritual. The last is the Pilgrim; the higher mental sheath which enfolds it from life to life bears the karmic imprints and so represents the karmic; the remaining "planes"—lower mental, astral, physical—are most influenced by the environing social and material world, being the arenas of greatest interplay between them and the pilgrimage "causal" body come into the world, and they represent the social self.

We have come out on Pilgrimage from the spiritual realm, retaining always a spark or ray of its eternal light within, and have dwelt and will dwell again in many worlds, some only intuitive, mental, or astral. After death the Pilgrim alone, bearing the karmic residue of a lifetime together with traces of many others, will return to astral and mental (Devachan) existence for a time before seeking incarnation again.

In early adulthood, however, after the storms of adolescence have been ridden out, ideally the karmic self will have somewhat subsided, its passions spent or channeled into family and vocation. Yet the same high weather is likely also to have obscured the Pilgrim, and one may think less about who one is alone. The social self more and more takes the helm. That is not bad, save that this self is likely to be especially vulnerable to the parasitic spiritual fantasies that hover around the material world it is now set to conquer, and it is easily confused or even conquered by them instead.

Yet in the years of the sun in strength, the task is to explore and experience the world of physical embodiment in all its fullness. Not in ways incompatible with the supreme imperatives of wisdom, love, and duty, but rather by tracking them through the mazes of matter as one can also on the planes of feeling and mind. This means, however, that the great Path may indeed be now taking us through the experiencing of the innocent joys of the flesh—of food and drink, of marriage, sexuality, and child-rearing, of art and music, of travel and sport, of the vibrancy and delight of flesh itself when it is at the peak of its power. There is nothing wrong with that, for it is all among the treasures of learning which we will bring with us upon our ultimate return to the Halls of Light, where all will be assimilated and understood.

True spirituality posits no cheap degrading of flesh and matter—which are expressions of God no less than mind and spirit—nor any radical dualism between them. Rather, it sees each as a completion of the other, and through wisdom holds them in balance. Undue partiality toward either the flesh or the higher spirit, at the expense of the other, leads to blindness in the other eye and is no more than arrogance of the ego-will striving to prove its power by warring against its own nature; time and time again such presumption has led to spiritual—or physical—disaster in the end. As the Isha Upanishad says, in a mysterious passage:

> To darkness are they doomed who devote themselves only to life in the world, and to a greater darkness they who devote themselves only to meditation . . . To darkness are they doomed who worship only the body, and to greater darkness they who worship only the spirit . . . They who worship both the body and the spirit, by the body overcome death, and by the spirit achieve immortality.[1]

All this is particularly pertinent to the world of young adulthood, the best season of all for the worship of the body together with the spirit.

Caution, however, is in order. Though the Path may be guiding one's destiny even when one's mind is elsewhere, it is well that it not be entirely forgotten amid the many demands and new experiences of young adulthood. For while life is meant now to be lived in the context of this cycle, it is not wholly of this cycle. The Path is still there, even when it is forgotten. But it wants to grow within you, and it slips you reminders of its presence. It yearns to let you know how you are faring on that endless and inward road, just as you mark milestones of vocational and family life. But its memoranda come in quite a different way than those.

Perhaps, in the midst of the highest, most celebrative events of the radiant years—weddings, successes, the coming of a child—there are those moments when you want to just sit still, taking it all in, uniting it all in your mind. Then, perhaps, there will come a sense without words: This is a timeless moment, not a moment of this time. This is an initiation, not for now only. All things have a larger significance, know it or not. I am in eternity too, and this joy is of eternity. Likewise, amid the sorrows and the pain—in their midst a kenning, fully realized consciously or not: something has been learned, a price has been paid, I am going past something I had to pass but now must go on—the road is long, longer than I can now know; move on.

And the Path can burst in more dramatically as well. Richard Bucke, in his classic work *Cosmic Consciousness,* tells this of himself:

> It was in the early spring at the beginning of his thirty-sixth year. He and two friends had spent the evening reading Wordsworth, Shelley, Keats, Browning, and especially Whitman. They parted at midnight, and he had a long drive in a hansom (it was in an English city). His mind deeply under the influence of the ideas, images and emotions called up by the reading and talk of the evening, was calm and peaceful. He was in a state of quiet, almost passive enjoyment. All at once, without warning of any kind, he found himself wrapped around as it were by a flame colored cloud. For an instant he thought of fire, some sudden conflagration in the great city, the next he knew that the light was within himself. Directly afterwards came upon him a sense of exultation, of immense joyousness accompanied or immediately followed by an intellectual illumination quite impossible to describe. Into his brain streamed one momentary lightning-flash of the Brahmic Splendor which has ever since lightened

his life; upon his heart fell one drop of Brahmic Bliss, leaving thence forward for always an after taste of heaven. Among other things he did not come to believe, he saw and knew that the Cosmos is not dead matter but a living Presence, that the soul of man is immortal, that the universe is so built and ordered that without any peradventure all things work together for the good of each and all, that the foundation principle of the world is what we call love and that the happiness of every one is in the long run absolutely certain . . . The illumination itself continued not more than a few moments, but its effects proved ineffaceable; it was impossible for him ever to forget what he at that time saw and knew, neither did he, or could he, ever doubt the truth of what was then presented to his mind. There was no return that night or at any other time of the experience . . .[2]

Bucke goes on to contend that his age at the time, the early to mid thirties, is the time when many of the world's greatest spiritual figures had their most decisive experiences, and that they, too, had in some way an experience of blinding, overwhelming light, that like his somehow gave absolute certainty of the reality and goodness of God and the universe. Bucke points to the enlightenment of the Buddha, the transfiguration and resurrection of Jesus, the most powerful mystical experiences of Paul, Plotinus, Muhammad (who was forty at the time of his first illumination), and Dante, among others.

I, too, had my most unforgettable mystical experience at the age of thirty-two. I had been meditating very quietly in a Spiritualist vein, when suddenly without warning a brilliant image of the sun appeared before my mental eye. I could think of nothing else; I could not move. Finally it faded slightly, and wispy clouds seemed to move across it, and tiny objects like planets or spaceships seemed to revolve around it, and then it finally passed from my inner vision. But so strong was the event that I could not stir from the chair in which I was sitting for nearly an hour afterwards— not wanting to move, read, speak—until my ordinary life had gathered itself back together. The experience seemed good, deeply though not passionately blissful, and above all profoundly meaningful though on some level beyond or apart from words. I have been trying to understand it more and more fully ever since, feeling that this was meant to be something of a lifetime task.

Set these spiritual illuminations against the temptations of midlife. Being in the fullness of life, we want to achieve what we can, to show the plenitude of our wit and our power. The monetary, status, and sexual symbols of life in the world seem as adequate as any for the purpose, for this is the hour when they seem most real. At the peak of power, when the reckoning seems far away, even death can be half laughed at as only another price to be paid. We may listen to the voice of Iago in Shakespeare's *Othello*:

> . . . Therefore put money in thy purse. If thou wilt needs damn thyself, do it a more delicate way than drowning. Make all the money thou canst. If sanctimony and a frail vow betwixt an erring barbarian and a super subtle Venetian be

not too hard for my wits and all the tribe of
hell, thou shalt enjoy her. Therefore make money.
A pox of drowning thyself! It is clean out of
the way. Seek thou rather to be hanged in com-
passing thy joy than to be drowned and go with-
out her.

But the reckoning does come, as Othello remarks at
the end, despite the difficulty of the midlife male to
shed tears or coddle emotion and sentimentality. After
killing his wife Desdemona and just before stabbing
himself in remorse, he realizes the guilt was not hers:

I have done the state some service, and they know't.
No more of that. I pray you, in your letters,
When you shall these unlucky deeds relate,
Speak of me as I am. Nothing extenuate,
Nor set down aught in malice. Then must you speak
Of one that loved not wisely, but too well;
Of one not easily jealous, but, being wrought,
Perplexed in the extreme; of one whose hand
. . . threw a pearl away
Richer than all his tribe; of one whose subdued eyes,
Albeit unused to the melting mood,
Drop tears as fast as the Arabian trees
Their medicinal gum.

For there is strength, in one so unused to the passions
of sentiment and remorse—the strong, silent type—in
being only able to swing when one does so with the
wholeness of an Othello. Find and use this strength in
young adulthood, adding to it the sensitivity gained as
one who is aware of the Path, and who can listen to its
whispers even in the course of busy days. Moreover, in
these years the Path may itself powerfully remind you

that it is still there, as we have seen. It will remind you that you have a character brought in from other lifetimes and other worlds, and what is even now being sowed will bear fruit in other lifetimes and in other worlds. It is well to have touchstones which remind you of your farther horizons. Maintain some symbol and some practice that keeps you in touch with the Path, and turn the mind to it from time to time.

This will, at first, be continuing in young adulthood whatever you have gained of Awakening, and whatever you have built of steady practice in the Preparative or Purgative Way. If you have begun the habit of any kind of prayer or meditation, any sort of participation in organized religion, keep it up.

If you have not yet begun, heed the voices that whisper inwardly in the highest and lowest moments of adult life. See what direction they seem to say you ought to follow to make your own connection with the Path. There is nothing wrong with encouraging an Awakening. Pursue what you inwardly see and hear. The distinguished mythologist Joseph Campbell said, "Follow your bliss." That is, follow your *own* way to spiritual realization, whatever it may be—you will know it by the fact that this way makes you happier than any other. Just thinking about it, just doing even the most routine practices of that way, makes you joyous, blissful—while other techniques may seem boring and forced. Follow your bliss—follow the path that is right to lead you onto the great Path, whatever it is: Zen, yoga, martial arts, bhakti, chanting a mantra, sitting quietly in the yard or in a park one day a week, or being active and worshiping in a conventional church or temple or coven. Or one of the many, many other ways that are now about and abroad in the world. There is one that's right for you, and you'll know it when you find it. It will bring you bliss; follow that bliss all the way home.

Setting foot on this path, cut the purgative channels deeper. Realize that the point of a single definite practice, such as a method of meditation, is to stop the activity of the stream of consciousness. Zen calls this the "monkey mind," because it jumps from one thought to another, like a monkey leaping from branch to branch. The monkey mind can be stopped by bringing it up against the stone wall of some definite practice which holds consciousness to a single point—the chant, the meditation focus, the liturgy, the yoga asana. Then you can begin to explore pure consciousness itself, to find the ocean of consciousness—personal, and beyond it cosmic—beneath the waves of rising and falling thought. You can let the mind take a vacation, and find out what mind is when it is not thinking about anything in particular. Stopping the monkey and getting into the realms of pure consciousness will give you a sense of a whole different way of being in the world, even as a young adult, and will offer a quiet, subtle form of bliss that will lead you on. For pure consciousness opens out in back, so to speak, onto the Path.

And along those deep irrigation channels sooner or later flowers will appear. They become beauty Paths. This is the dawning of the Illuminative stage, when you can begin to find deep satisfaction in religious and spiritual life. Prayers are answered, feelings of the presence of God and the rapture of profound intercommunion with the divine may be frequent, and meditation can lead to a rich inner peace of mind. Your spiritual life can become a staple of everyday routine. These rewards flourish in the soil of the spirit first uncovered at the Awakening, and then cultivated and watered by the regular practice of the Purgative stage. As Teresa of Avila put it, the seeds planted at the beginning of the spiritual adventure now burst into bloom. And these flowers may be of many different varieties.

For there are many paths within the Illuminative Path. Evelyn Underhill calls it a way within the Way, for it has its own little ordeals, progresses, and victories. Some souls may emphasize prayer, finding their fulfillment in a rich interpersonal life with God. Theoreticians of bhakti within the Hindu tradition, like devotees in many other faiths, have discovered that there are many stages in the path of prayer itself.

You may begin feeling very small and insecure before the awesome power of the Almighty, making petitions as a respectful servant to a master, or as a child before loving but seemingly huge and omnipotent parents who can reward or punish, or favor or ignore for reasons of their own. But even the most disparate relationship can become less intimidating, easier, with experience. In time master and servant or parent and child can mellow to the familiarity of friend and friend, as you learn to carry on colloquial, even joking, conversations with God in your heart, laying out all joys and sorrows, problems and puzzlements, before your Companion. Finally the relationship deepens to the intimacy of lover and beloved, a passionate seizing on the presence of the other as the foundation and joy of your life, the delight without which all is desolate. It is no longer so much a matter of asking God for anything; the closeness of God is enough. In a poignant and profound insight, bhaktas tell us that even the absence of God is a confirmation of divine love. For like a human lover God seems occasionally not to be there, as though testing the lover or even providing reward in some enigmatic way. Yet at such times even the abysmal yearning and despair you know is proof of God's reality and enduring love.

Others may be led to God more through the experience of meditation, realizing the Creator less as the loving Other than as a divine sea met and merged within the depths of your inwardness. Quiet the mind, let the monkey take a nap, and individual consciousness flows toward the universal. Here too there may be stages of awareness, though perhaps more subtle than those of the way of prayer and devotional love. At first you may naturally require a strong focus to keep the mind from wandering: counting breaths, a candle flame, a mantra, a powerful inner mental image of sacred significance. Finally the day may come when, at first gingerly and only briefly, you can take away that prop and experience a moment of pure, "unsupported" consciousness. In time you may be able to move in and out of this zestful empty fullness of pure consciousness freely.

The Illuminative stage may also be a time of congenial participation in the "conventional" religion of church and temple. If you are a young adult, marriage and a growing family may move you toward the social and spiritual support religious institutions can give. Yet there are inward reasons for this participation as well. The Illuminative ways are based upon times, places, methods, and images. We pray and meditate at certain times and in certain places, by and large not truly "without ceasing." We probably pray at first in accordance with certain learned forms or practices, even with certain postures like kneeling or Zen sitting. We think of God with the help of certain mental images, words of scripture, or artistic portrayals. We may find that music, from old-time hymns to chant, sends the soul heavenward as well.

Nothing is wrong with this for now, even though the soul may sometimes seem to strain against those forms for something wider and deeper. But in the Illuminative stage such aids are important as supports that meet us where we are as sensory and image-thinking beings. The right religious group may help us in many ways: it can provide familiar images and sensory experiences, set apart times and places for the practice of prayer and meditation, offer helpful teachings, and give us sympathetic friends to encourage us on the way.

I am not, however, saying that adherence to religious groups and teachers should be regarded as only provisional, something to be cast aside when you reach a more exalted level of spirituality. Individual paths differ, of course. But such an attitude can all too easily lead to the great fault of spiritual pride, of thinking your spirituality is something you have achieved by your own efforts and is now yours like a diploma. Serious perils lurk in waiting for the solitary seeker. Many of the most truly advanced souls—holy monks or lay world-servers, even saints and bodhisattvas—do not disdain active and humble worship with others in the services of their faith. For while they know God's presence is everywhere and everywhen, they also know that for this very reason God *is* in that worship, that its forms do create inner-plane channels for divine energy, and that by worshiping with others they provide support for them in their own Pathwalking.

For many, in fact, the Illuminative stage may appear to be what religion and spirituality are all about, and it is felt to be enough in terms of spiritual fulfillment. What more could you want than a richly satisfying inner life, the power and motivation to do good in the world, forms of worship which are agreeable to your soul, and a goodly fellowship of kindred souls around you? Yet the *Visudhamagga,* a major Buddhist treatise from the fifth century, speaks of a "pseudo-nirvana" in the middle stages of one's advancement in meditation. In the West, writers like John of the Cross talk of mystical bliss which *precedes* a new purgation, and a final nearness to God unimagined by the merely pious. This presages the subtle imperfections mixed into the glories of Illumination.

First, you are tempted to think that you have "arrived," that even God can lead no further. But that sort of contentment and self-satisfaction is deadly to real spirituality. In genuine spiritual attainment you are always emptying yourself, recognizing how much greater God is than anything you can imagine. This humility is not degradation or agonizing over real or imagined sins; it is quite different from that, and not at all incompatible with deep joy and love. The truly spiritual just experience the love and joy without worrying about the self who is experiencing them, above all not becoming inflated with that self's spiritual status. This is like a lover, who even while experiencing all the joys of love, still is full of wonder that the beloved should bestow so much upon him or her.

Second, in the Illuminative state one can become attached to spiritual experiences as pleasures, and even become a glutton for them, as another might for food or drink. You want and need more and more, until prayer and meditation become ends in themselves, not merely means to better know God and serve humanity. In the process you may become fascinated with your spiritual life, making it a sort of hobby or obsession, and you are always taking your spiritual temperature and measuring your progress. All this too easily becomes something quite other than simply self-emptying yourself before the Infinite.

Finally, the Illuminative stage still retains a separation between the spiritual life and the rest of life. As we have seen, it has its distinctive and privileged times, places, means, and images. This is normal, even though religion also strives to overcome all separateness, until the world is like the heavenly city described in the Book of Revelation, without temple because the glory of God is everywhere in it. Yet if certain situations are marked off as especially religious, it implies that others are less so and far from God. But if the divine Reality is unconditioned, how can anywhere, even the subtlest thought, be apart from God? In the end this tension must be resolved.

Again, for some, the Illuminative way may be enough, at least for this lifetime. That is not to be scorned; many wonderful and godly persons have known no more than its ways and paths. Others, however, may in time register a call to something else. The Purgative way is a time of digging deep channels to direct water from the springs of Awakening. In the Illuminative way, those canals are filled and flowers bloom along their banks. But now there comes a time, for those so called, when the banks must be made level and the waters become a shoreless sea. Adrift on that sea, the Pilgrim will learn that all waves and foaming breakers are full to bursting with God, that you can no more gluttonously hold on to God than you can a handful of water, and that you never "arrive" on this particular journey because the sea is endless in all directions, though the wandering voyage amid billows of love and joy is well worthwhile, indeed the only thing truly worthwhile. Before that wonder arises, however, the rudders must be made firm so the voyage can be well navigated. So, amidst the beauties of Illumination, the aspirant may be cast ashore. The bubbling billows turn dry. The old ways and old joys are no more, and all seems dust and dryness. One is cast up high and dry on the desert of the Dark Night, there to train for embarkation on the shoreless sea of the Unitive state.

Young adulthood is a time for taking in the Illuminative stage, but in a way that will best prepare one to move on, however adventurous and difficult the next stage of the journey may be. As we have seen, the high emotions, perceptions, and obligations of young adulthood all offer excellent contexts for spiritual Illumination. That is well; go for it—or rather let it come to you freely. But remember also that this stage is not final; nothing that comes to you is more than another image; in the end it will go as freely as it has come. Swim in it like a swimmer in a sparkling river, pulling with the stream but with open hands.

Remember to keep the fundamentals of life natural, to keep with the basics of life: flesh and blood, birth and death, wholesome simple food and drink, without letting parasitic symbols or illusions twist them around. Go with the truly natural always. Let children grow up; let yourself change as nature means you to; those are sufficient signs that the stream flows on and more of the Path still lies ahead.

The Path will whisper: Keep on going. This was one way to Walk, the beauty part, but it was not the only way. Even from the highest peak you cannot see it all; there's more to come, pleasant and painful, and beyond pleasure and pain, more than you can now imagine. Keep on going.

# The Demons and Delights of Midday:
## Middle Age

T hen comes the first surprise. The Pilgrim reaches midlife.

If life is like a journey, the middle years may seem like a portion of that long expedition which passes through desert terrain, such as that of the American Southwest. I hasten to add this does not mean it is all bad. There are those who love desert landscapes, with their sharp austere beauty, the finely nuanced reds and browns of rock and soil, the far horizons and azure skies of day and the seemingly countless cold, bright, unimaginably distant stars by night.

But deserts can also be monotonous, and wells of fresh water are far to seek. In middle age one day can seem very much the same as another. The truly exciting moments that make certain days stand out brilliantly —one's first day in college, one's first day in a foreign country, wedding bells, the first day on a job, the day a child is born—all these are likely to be secured in the past with silver locks, and memory the only key. The children are grown and away from home, the job has long since grown routine, the marriage, even if still basically good, is also routine. Like a desert landscape, life in the middle years keeps going about the same mile after mile, and little refreshment is at hand. Even the games, the travels, the entertainments no longer sparkle as in the days of youth, and there are times when life seems nothing but a weary road into the sunset. But deserts offer spectacular sunsets and painted rocks and rills too, and the incredibly gorgeous night sky. Middle age has their equivalents as well.

The most appealing middle aged people I know are easy to be with, and they have a soft, wise twinkle in their eyes. They live their lives and do their jobs, quietly and efficiently. They also have time just to be, and to look. They have looked enough to know the world is not quite what it pretends to be, and the real meaning is in code. Fortunately, that code is not hard to crack. You may break it without even exactly knowing that's what you're doing. It doesn't take mathematical or cryptographic skills, but only the ability to look carefully and lovingly into the faces and the dramas of all beings, in this and all other worlds.

You will see beauty in ordinary things, like the beauty in the tinted red rocks of the desert that might at first be overlooked. You will see the far beauty encoded in memory and hope, like that of the thronging distant stars that follow the desert sunset, and you will know that each being is really a star that will set only to rise again over a fresh horizon. Knowing this, one can do three things at once: love, care, and smile.

The slow, repetitious days of middle age are ideal for looking, and then for loving, caring, and smiling. Enough passion has been spent that one can often just simply see, without everything being distorted by heat-waves. It is no longer necessary to respond with flaming anger, giddy joy, or coarse lust to every provocation. By now it is possible to just be aware of the provocation and the feeling, acknowledge it, but set it aside in favor of a calm assessment of the situation and its possibilities, and then act or not act accordingly. Some would call that maturity, and some burnout. I say that if one is freed to look through the passion to love, care, and smile, that is the essence of maturity and even more. Passion spent, the variety and the ordinariness of life can return and find room to flourish, and in them there is much to love, to care about, to smile at—in middle age there is the time and the space to do so. But some middle agers learn this lesson sooner than others.

What is really going on here? First, recall again the stages of the spiritual life, as presented by Evelyn Underhill: Awakening, Purgation, Illumination, the Dark Night of the Soul, and the Unitive state. I have postulated that these stages may have a correlation in the spirituality of the different natural periods of a human life, from youth to maturity. I would now like to suggest that middle age, seen spiritually, is like a "natural" Dark Night of the Soul, and if well passed through, can open one to the Unitive state in old age. I have noted before that life is a series of natural as well as "programmed" initiations. It should not be surprising, then, that middle age can correspond to a "natural" experience of the Dark Night of the Soul, when all seems murky and the splendor of God's presence, as we perhaps once knew it, seems withdrawn. Spiritual writers have spoken of the "demons of midday," corrosive foes that attack when life seems to be moving toward its peak, when all is sunny and going well. They attack obscurely and from within, just as night—in cluding the Dark Night—first begins in the unnoticed shadowy corners.

But what does all this mean for one in midlife? Deny the Dark Night? Now after middle age and meeting the demons of midday, you cannot go back to the Illuminative state and youthful exaltations as though nothing has happened. You can never really go back, either in the life of the spirit or of the flesh. But you can move on in unexpected ways. Let it happen, but be sure of how you are moving. These are restless years of metaphysical wanderlust. They are the years of the celebrated midlife crisis, when not a few of us, ultimately yearning no doubt for a recovery of lost youth, commence thinking of adding spice to a hopelessly humdrum home life by exchanging the present spouse for another, presumably a younger and more attractive model. We may toy with the notion of making a midcourse career change, leaving a calling such as accounting, which has long since become terminally routine, for something more exciting, anywhere from archaeology to zoology. Not all such vocational changes are necessarily bad. Few would fault Albert Schweitzer for giving up a secure academic position to become a medical missionary in Africa, with all that his example has meant to the world.

But we need to consider of what stuff the demons of midday are made. Underneath the restlessness lies a fresh and probably unexpected, perhaps unwanted, but demanding uncertainty—uncertainty about who one is, where one is supposed to be, who one is supposed to be with, what one really believes. These demons are very tough, persistent fellows, and they have a one-track mind. All they need to accomplish is to sow doubt. No answers—just doubt, doubt, over and over. Doubt about everything. That's all it takes. This makes one itchy, unhappy, angry, ready for surrogate answers in book, bed, or bottle, and it makes the Path look very, very dim—hardly a trace at all.

The basic doubt of course is spiritual doubt. If nothing is really true, or if nothing can really be known about God or Ultimate Reality, then everything is up for grabs. Religious and philosophical doubts can have a "ripple effect" on all the rest of one's life, raising inner questions about all one's beliefs and commitments. The doubts can really be there, wanted or not, and they don't all come from demons. You may by now have seen through most of the conventional arguments for the existence of God. You may have seen and experienced enough of the adult world to recognize a certain relativism in moral matters. After all, good people occasionally do bad things, and bad people do good things, and most of us are a mixture of both anyway. One must be compassionate as well as passionate, understanding as well as standing for things. As the French say, "To understand all is to forgive all," and there are things that you would like to understand and forgive in yourself, too.

But the question is again, where are you going with all of this? Our time in this life and this world is only moving in one direction, and there is only so much of it. Soon we will no longer be of interest even to the demons of midday, the sun having moved in our particular sky, and the demons will slink away toward new victims. The question to ask is whether the doubts, and the passion and compassion, are truly real or are a byproduct of spiritual chronology.

Doubt is not a sin, and at the right time and in the right context, it may be the result of the most sterling intellectual honesty. Nor is it a sin to reassess one's commitments, if doing so seems mandated by even higher spiritual and moral imperatives than those which first sanctioned the commitments.

The question is, however, where midlife doubts, wavering, and charging off in new directions come from—perhaps they are less the fruit of the intellect than of changing spiritual stages, and they need to be viewed in that light. It may be that they are the winding down of the Illuminative stage and are signs of the Dark Night, and that the compass in that midday gloaming should be put aside rather than followed off in new campaigns.

All of the stages in the spiritual journey begin with a period of uncertainty, doubt, and confusion, and this is probably especially true of the Dark Night. Evelyn Underhill speaks of its onset as a time of "rapid oscillation" between joyous and painful consciousness. The mystics call this a "game of love" in which God plays, as it were, hide and seek with the soul.[1] In this condition, we are told, there is likely to be confusion, even a feeling of stupidity and childishness, as when you learn anything new—such as a new game or computer program. St. Teresa said that there were times during her Dark Night when she could not read and comprehend the simplest books, though they were in her native Spanish. The mystical Madame Guyon said of this time that "it is an amazing thing, for a soul that believed herself to be advanced in the way of perfection, when she sees herself thus go to pieces all at once." St. John of the Cross, the great master of discussion of the Dark

Night, confessed that the greatest affliction of it is the thought that God has abandoned you.

So it may be, and undoubtedly a sense of divine abandonment lies at the very core of the distress of midday and midlife. But for many of us who are not as consciously religious as the saint, that awareness may take veiled rather than conscious form. Instead of thinking of God, we may think only, "My life is falling apart," "Nothing seems to mean anything any-more," "I'm not sure of anything; it's all messed up." But what are such sentiments as these but realizations that you have lost connection with the interrelatedness and central direction of the universe, which some call God? And what is it, also, but a sense that you have gotten out of touch with the Path?

The old spiritual writers of the West had a term, accidie (acedia), for a sort of combined lethargy and quiet depression which monks and others all too easily fall into after their first zeal has worn off. The state was sometimes spoken of, in the language of Psalm 91, as "the sickness that destroyeth in the noon-day." It is not a colorful or dramatic sin, but like a persistent low-grade fever can in the end be very dangerous, for it is a canker that gnaws away at a person's vitals until she or he is all hollow inside. It is the debilitating self-pity of Shakespeare's King Lear, as he cries, "You see me here, you gods, a poor old man, As full of grief as age; wretched in both . . . A poor, infirm, weak, and despis'd old man . . . unaccommodated man is no more but such a poor, bare, forked animal . . . I am bound upon a wheel of fire . . . I am a very foolish fond old man."

It is not so much great crimes of passion that many of us have to contend with as the years advance. Instead, it is the quiet sense of feeling your powers slip away very slowly, as do the years, so that climbing the stairs or handling the confusion at the office takes a bit more work. It is seeing your children grow and wondering if you are still really important or if anything really important can happen to you again, and if there can ever again be truly major events in your life such as marriage or childbirth. Like Lear, you may fondly and foolishly wonder if your daughters still love you and how that might be proven. It is the regrets and dreams, thinking of the lost opportunities and the long-past decisions that turned your life in one direction and can never be unmade, and of all the years that can never be relived.

All these are quiet things. But like poison working deep within your innards, they can envenom life with the acids of self-pity, self-doubt, and quiet despair. Life just no longer seems really worthwhile, and when it does not, the world grows gray. The image of the desert looms large, so like the "blasted heath" upon which Lear poured out the fullest blasts of his rage and pity. We may wonder why we are crossing this desert anyway. No doubt it is the shadows of the prison-house again.

A deeper understanding of the aspects of human nature may help clarify for us our need for transiting the desert and the Dark Night. As we have seen, we go into life with a complex heritage. Theosophy speaks of the sevenfold nature of humankind. There is the "Upper Triad," or the personal trinity comprised of the atma, or divine nature within; the buddhic nature, or the intuitive, creative "spiritual" soul; and the higher manas, or mind in its purest and most joyous aspect. This Upper Triad is always within and can always be touched by those who seek within, and in touching the seeker will meet with fire and fresh fountains of living water. It is also the "causal body" or that which ultimately reincarnates, and so carries the karmic imprints. We are also composed of the always-present and exceedingly useful "Lower Quaternity": the lower manas or mind in its ordinary problem-solving, remembering, forgetting, plain everyday thinking aspect; prana or the "Astral Body" which dwells on higher or lower levels of the watery worlds of dreams, fancies, feelings, and emotions; the etheric body which is like a pattern and subtle-matter double of the physical body; and finally the physical body itself.

Although sometimes called planes, it must be understood that these seven aspects of human nature interpenetrate and flow in and out of each other. We may shift our attention from one to another with the ease and speed of a flying thought. One moment we may be grossly physical, the next virtually divine in our inner life. Dreams are often virtual excursions into the astral world, where desires and fears create ephemeral forms to fulfill themselves as easily as they are thought.

As we move more and more through life, we identify more fully with the Lower Quaternity. This material world is where the action is, so to speak. Physicality, feelings, fancies, memories, and the occasional rational thought are what make the world go 'round. This is the level at which we spend a good deal of our time, in order to keep up with the world. There is the attractiveness of that person, my dream of a condo at the ski resort, my loathing for that politician's rhetoric, how I can't get that foolish thing I did as a teenager out of my mind, and so on. I try to meet that attractive person, I sacrifice a lot—maybe including some ethical principles—for the money to buy the condo dream, I support the other political party. Many others follow the same circle, and the world keeps going 'round. In effect, we put the Upper Triad in cold storage. Then we wonder why our lives seem to be getting more and more dry and empty, why we have lost the sense of poetry and inspiration we may once have had. We ask, is God, or at least our own god, dead, or perhaps asleep?

To make things worse, we are not talking about our own inner nature alone. Above all in modern civilization, we are surrounded by millions of others more or less like us, and their "vibes," karmic waves, astral desire-forms—whatever they may be called—fill the inner-planes' "space" of earth and cluster around us, sometimes as parasites seeking entry.

We know about pollution in the physical environment: smog, noise, litter, pesticides, electrical pulsations, fluorides depleting the ozone layer. The same civilization also fills the psychic space of our planet with the droppings, impulses, and demonic mutants stemming from all its greed, its depraved desires, its psychic epidemics. There are also, of course, benign channels opened by good thoughts and saintly souls through which we can move if we have the skill or guidance.

In any case, we are not alone. As we forget the divine within and the Upper Triad, and try to steer blind by uncertain feeling and bare unaided reason, or even just by physical drive, we are in no position to fend off psychic hitchhikers and hijackers very well. We don't even have the larger vision, accessible only through the high manas and the rest of the Higher Triad, to know about or understand such things in their true nature, and to see them for what they are. We are bombarded by often unwholesome psychic influences all the time, but we may know them no more than might a city under siege that takes the enemy's missiles only for shooting stars, even as they hit and destroy houses. We are talking, of course, about the kind of troubled spiritual parasites in the mind that masquerade as good material pleasures—food, drink, sex, comfort—but are twisted so as to cater to distorted fantasy forms thereof rather than the healthy natural version. Regrettably, much in crowded modern civilization has actually only caused population explosions on the astral as well as the physical plane. While there is much that is good in the modern city, there is also much that is not what it seems, but is clouded by psychic smog and that which breeds it and breeds in it. Amid its dank miasmas, the imps of deception flit about just outside mind and sight, but curve the air to cause moral double vision nonetheless, preying on all those whose eye is not single.

In the later years of midlife of which we are speaking, we may be particularly vulnerable to psychic parasites. We become weary of constant spiritual struggle, and the first energy of spiritual enthusiasm is gone. As we experience more and more of life and its people we may see things that encourage a greater degree of ethical doubt as the only way to compassion and worldly wisdom. Also our own drives demand their due, and we are inclined toward the kind of wisdom that wants to be no less than forgiving of ourselves; this "wisdom" tells us that to deny ourselves our desires is an unhealthy repression. We forget how to be in the world without being of the world. Drawn to an unhealthy desire for, say, alcohol, unsafe and inappropriate sex, or money, we may say that this is only human nature, despite the fact that what we are doing is destructive of that same human nature, with all the hallmarks of a passionate need to fulfill some fancy we don't really need for any legitimate human end, but which has burned itself into our brain. The image may be of drink as a symbol of conviviality or inward well-being that we think we can't achieve without it; of a sexually desirable person who becomes like an obsession in our dreams; or money (itself pure abstract symbol), and the ego-enhancement of living a lifestyle that it can buy. Yet we know in some corner of our minds that these things are as likely to destroy us—physically, socially, spiritually or all three—as to deliver any of what they promise. Why are they then so hard to let go of? Is it our own twisted nature? Or the pervasive influence of an all-pervasive corrupt society? Or is it perhaps psychic parasites who can only fulfill their own lower desires through us, then toss us aside like empties? Theosophy is not dogmatic about such answers, but does not rule out any of them either. All three, it seems to me, illumine some aspect of the mystery of iniquity in human life.

Whatever the reason for our seeming need for self-destruction, it becomes harder to avoid as we get older and slog our way further and further from the sunrise. Life may seem more and more like a desert—full of ghosts. But remember, people visit the desert for two reasons: They can be there just because they have to get across it. And they can be there because there is something they want to find, and the desert is the best place to look for it. The desert may be the Dark Night of the Soul. In its cleanness and purity, it may also be the way out of the Dark Night—it is far from the parasites under city streetlights, far from videos and voices.

All through history, deserts have attracted prophets, mystics, seekers after God of all kinds:  Moses at the Burning Bush; Paul going into the desert after his conversion; the "Desert Fathers" of early Christianity; Hindu sadhus on pilgrimage to Kailas, the mount of Shiva in the windy wastes of Tibet; Native Americans on the Vision Quest. It is not that God is necessarily more in the desert than anywhere else. But there is much less in the desert to distract one from God. As an Eskimo shaman told the explorer Knut Rasmussen, "All true wisdom is only to be found far from men, out in the great solitude, and it can only be acquired by suffering."[2] The Svetasvatara Upanishad of ancient India tells the aspirant to:

> Retire to a solitary place, such as a mountain cave or a sacred spot. The place must be protected from the wind and rain, and it must have a smooth, clean floor, free from pebbles and dust. It must not be damp, and it must be free from disturbing noises. It must be pleasing to the eye and quieting to the mind. Seated there, practice meditation and other spiritual exercises.[3]

The Desert Fathers of the early Christian church, living as religious hermits on the deserts of Egypt in the waning days of the Roman Empire, experienced the world from a radically different perspective than most of us. St. Jerome, in "The Life of St. Paul the First Hermit," tells of that ascetic who spent a hundred and thirteen years living "the life of heaven upon earth" utterly alone in an oasis so tiny it consisted of only a spring, a garden, and a single palm tree. When he was at long last visited by another famous hermit, the scarcely less venerable St. Antony, Paul asked his guest the news, yet not without some trepidation since then as now the tidings were often discouraging: "Yet because love endureth all things, tell me, I pray thee, how fares the human race: if new roofs be risen in the ancient cities, whose empire is it that now sways the world; and if any still survive, snared in the error of the demons."[4] But Paul's true life was elsewhere than this earth; soon after, hurrying back to visit him again, Antony, in a vision, saw his friend "climbing the steps of heaven, and shining white as snow." When he arrived, he found only the lifeless body of St. Paul.

For some of us, literal retirement to the desert may not be possible, although it is possible to arrange a few days at a monastery or other retreat center or, if you are a backpacker or have a camper, to plan your own time of spiritual renewal in the wilderness. You may be surprised at your own awakening "in the desert." You can also create a private desert, in the positive sense, around you. The idea is to cut the rate of psychic bombardment by lower vibes, and to give yourself time and space to get in touch again with the divine and the true higher self within the Upper Triad. The positive desert is a clean pure space where the air is clear and the stars are bright, on all planes. This clarity is like a ring of protection against bombardment, and a channel through which the light of atma, buddhi, and higher manas can shine to irradiate your whole being.

How do you maintain your desert? The best way is to start a spiritual practice during the time of isolation and retreat—whether literally in the desert, at a monastery or retreat house, or on a quiet day at home—and then to practice it, morning and evening, under the breath throughout the day, after you return. You could try the Tibetan Buddhist *Om mani padme hum* ("One—the jewel in the lotus—the many"; capable of interpretation on many esoteric levels), or the Christian *Gloria Patri* ("Glory be to the Father, and to the Son, and to the Holy Spirit"), or just the syllable One, over and over. One really says it all: One God, One Reality behind all the forms, One Path uniting all the paths. Let these inner words, nearer than breath, pervade your life, till they resound like a symphony heard only by you to accompany your goings out and your comings in.

Symphonies have something in common with sunrises and sunsets. They can open up new feelings and new expectations we hardly knew we had before. A wordless, ageless sense of wonder and beauty can come over you before the audial beauty of the One and the visual beauty of the Two. But now, as life advances and deepens toward the west, we are looking at sunsets. Yet out of the beauty of that inner harmony may come a stilling of all ruffled airs and the Unitive colors of sundown may appear.

## Sunset and Evening Star:
### The Beauty of Old Age

*Sunset and evening star,*
*And one clear call for me!*
*And may there be no moaning of the bar,*
*When I put out to sea.*

*But such a tide as moving seems asleep,*
*Too full for sound and foam,*
*When that which drew from out the boundless deep*
*Turns again home.*

*Twilight and evening bell,*
*And after that the dark!*
*And may there be no sadness of farewell,*
*When I embark;*

*For tho' from out our bourne of Time and Place*
*The flood may bear me far,*
*I hope to see my Pilot face to face*
*When I have crost the bar.*

—Crossing the Bar, *Alfred, Lord Tennyson*

I s it really true that old people, having passed through the Illuminative stage of young adulthood, and the Dark Night of the Soul of middle age, are in the Unitive state?

Well, yes and no. As we have noted, not all elderly people appear to be highly advanced spiritually, and some may appear to regress to childish, petty, and otherwise unpleasant conditions unworthy of them in their best moments, much less of anything like sainthood. Others may show little sign of ever having grown much spiritually in the course of a long life. Often the deplorable spirit of an elderly person can and must be understood in terms of physical, psychological, or other causes outside of the patient's control which can only be forgiven, and the person remembered as she or he was in the crowning years. Sometimes, persons seem deliberately to refuse to mature in any way, dying as selfish and spiteful as they were apparently born or even becoming hardened in evil as the years roll by.

On the other hand, most of us have known elderly persons of rare beauty. Inwardly they are letting go of the world, while maintaining love for the entities large and small within it, and manifesting a sense of living in the present. An elderly person of great spiritual radiance can have a remarkable impact on those of all ages. We want, we yearn for, the wise old woman and wise old man, the senior mother or father of much experience and much wisdom, the seasoned sage and saint, the guru and guide, the master and mahatma; we sense that, after the primary responsibilities of life have been attended to, one has at last opportunity to grow much in love, wisdom, and interiority; we want to be in touch with those who seem to have taken that opportunity.

This is really the point. It is not that all old people are in the Unitive state. It is not that you must be elderly to be in it. (If traditional accounts of their lives are to be believed, some saints like Ramakrishna were virtually born in it; some like St. Rose of Lima achieved it as teenagers.) It is simply that in age, after having been prepared by the earlier stages of life, you have a special opportunity to crown your life with the Unitive state, *if* your inner disposition is set for it, and *if* you are able to resist those remaining temptations that stand in its way.

The Unitive state means that your consciousness is largely united to that of God, or to Brahman, the universal ground of Being; to the Dao, the great Path down which all things flow, or to the Buddha-nature, the way a buddha sees the world in the moment of enlightenment. It does not mean that you have infinite knowledge, magical powers, or anything like that. It does not mean you are never mistaken about anything, never make wrong moral or factual judgments, or never have feelings—depression or anger or whatever—supposedly unworthy of a saint. It does not mean that you are always *conscious* of God, always thinking rapturously of God's love. The true deep spirituality of the highest states is beyond words or ideas, and above heavy emotional feelings however ecstatic. One is so close to God there is no place for language, so closely identified with God no space remains for the waves of love, unless on the deepest and subtlest level—"too full for sound and foam."

The best way I know how to positively put what this means is to say that the Unitive saint is completely *natural*—nature as it is at its truest—illumined from within by the glory of the Eternal, which it manifests in changing form. The Unitive saint is simply a natural human being, and allows no obstacle to come between her or his everyday life and the nature of things at the ground of Being. It is, after all, natural to be calm, and loving, and to radiate beauty; plants, animals, and babies do this without being taught. It is also natural once in a while to be angry or upset. The Unitive saint does all this with the grace and resilience of nature itself; where, as says old Laozi in the Daodejing, a sapling tree pulled all the way down to the ground will spring back up when released, and the wind does not need to blow more than half a day. Being one with the universe, the Unitive life is one with the ebb and flow of its tides, and with the joy of their play.

In age there is time and encouragement to develop this mind. The psychology of the aging person is more conducive to it than ever before. In age there are perhaps fewer crossgrained distractions than when jobs are hectic and children are young. One is naturally inclined to take things more slowly, to want less and demand less, save the good of one's children (of the flesh or of the spirit)—and thus to approach the state of God, who wants nothing because everything is already possessed, save what is desired because of love and sorrow for the world.

Above all, the aging person begins to see life and time like God: all pasts as present. One begins to know by some sort of inner temporal sense that the pasts one remembers, over increasingly many years, are not lost or gone, but simply not what is now called the present; they are only in some other place, as real and eternally as real as ever. The flowers and snows of yesterday are

there; so are the streets and cities, the loves and chil-
dren, as they were then and are eternally in the eye
of God. The sad things too, the losses and mistakes
and shames and cruelties of one's life, they are there as
well, but now just to be seen till they are seen through,
understood and dismissed. And as things are seen by
the eye of God, so are they seen and so they are to the
Unitive saint who sees through the eye of God. All this
an aging person begins to understand, though it is hard
to explain.

Even in age, one does not simply slide into the
Unitive state. There are temptations: despondency and
forgetfulness of the Path. The two are closely related.
Depression is a steady assailant of old age, as we have
seen in the case of King Lear. There is much to encour-
age it. Even though in some ways life may be simpler in
retirement and with the children gone, in other ways
it may often be harder. Illnesses, arthritis, and the plain
tiredness that come with years may make tasks as com-
monplace as opening a can or taking a trip to the doc-
tor major productions. You forget things. The house or
apartment seems quiet and hollow with the family out
and on its own. People you knew well, perhaps those
nearest and dearest, die and leave an empty chair. Well-
meaning younger relatives, friends, and nurses talk to
older people as though they were children and treat
them that way. It can hardly seem worthwhile to go on.

Here is where two things that older people can do
very well are helpful. One is taking one day at a time,
which is the other side of seeing all times as real and,
from an ultimate point of view, as One. For if that is the
case, and with most responsibilities now in the past,
why not live in the present? The other is remembering

the Path. Let the present stretch out in both directions, so to speak, to be the path winding its way through this and all other lives on the great Pilgrimage. The present moment, although you are in old age, is as important as any other, because it is the Path, and the Path goes on—through life in all its stages, through death and life again. Nothing is all-important or unimportant to it; it all comes together. All the stages of your life, now held in memory, come together to be the Path in this life, and the foundation of the next. There is nothing to worry about, and everything to live for.

We can contemplate with composure the dissolution of one temporality, affirming with Prospero in Shakespeare's *The Tempest*:

> . . . Be cheerful, sir.
> Our revels now are ended. These our actors,
> As I foretold you, were all spirits and
> Are melted into air, into thin air:
> And, like the baseless fabric of this vision,
> The cloud-capp'd towers, the gorgeous palaces,
> The solemn temples, the great globe itself,
> Yea, all which it inherit, shall dissolve
> And, like this insubstantial pageant faded,
> Leave not a rack behind. We are such stuff
> As dreams are made on, and our little life
> Is rounded with a sleep.

Then comes the most remarkable scene in this late play of Shakespeare's, perhaps intended as the Bard's climaxing message, when the wizard Prospero throws away his magic staff and book, saying "This rough magic I here abjure." He sets free Caliban and all others who were under his enchantment, preferring now to

live and be in the real ordinary world just as it is, with
no more than ordinary powers. When the play is over
the actors become who they really are, when the magic
is gone we see the world without glamorized colored
glasses, when the dream is done we wake up and smell
the coffee of genuine reality. Magic only replaces one
illusion with another; when you have cut through to
the hard core beneath the racks and clouds, you can
throw away the wands and spell-books.

This is the challenge and opportunity of old age:
when you've seen it all, to realize that you have and to
let go of all that which you now know is not as real as
it looks, to just hang out on the reality level. Just to be
a natural human being. To be, to know, and to love.

You will be one of those elders well recognized by
the young, who have wise eyes, who can be told every-
thing without fear, who can tell of understanding every-
thing with a silent smile, yet can also find the right
words to upbuild and correct without rancor. They have
in their faces the soft beauty of candlelight, and seem
to radiate a tender yet invincible calm within. Some-
how, you know that calm is not theirs alone, but is in
them because they are part of something larger that
over the years they have found or has come to them.

The psychologist Abraham Maslow is celebrated as
the father of humanistic psychology and explorer of
what he called the "peak experience" or "being state"
—those creative, ecstatic moments which seem to be
out of time and are comparable to the deepest mystical
experiences of saints and enlightened beings. But it
took the final years of Maslow's life for him to discover
something even better in some ways than the peak
experiences of young lovers and poets or ecstatic con-

templatives. For though less intense the experience was steady, pervasive, and of great power to free one from all fear. Maslow called it the "plateau experience"; it seems little different from the Unitive state. A very serious heart attack two years before his death brought Maslow to this high plain, which he also spoke of as his post-mortem life—his life after death:

> My attitude toward life changed. The word I use for it now is the post-mortem life. I could just as easily have died, so that my living constitutes a kind of an extra, a bonus . . . I might just as well live as if I had already died . . . Every single moment of every single day is transformed because the pervasive undercurrent—the fear of death—is removed.[1]

Putting together Maslow's incomplete descriptions of this final state attained toward the end of life, his biographer has summarized it in these words:

> [It is] a serene and calm, rather than intensely emotional, response to what we experience as miraculous or awesome. The high plateau always has a noetic and cognitive element, unlike the peak experience, which can be merely emotional; it is also far more volitional than the peak experience; for example, a mother who sits quietly gazing at her baby playing on the floor beside her.[2]

This state, we are further told, can be precipitated by certain positive things, such as looking at elevating art or listening to good music—or watching a child play on the floor. It can have its moments fuller than others. According to Maslow:

One very important aspect of the post-mortem life is that everything gets doubly precious, gets piercingly important. You get stabbed by things, by flowers and by babies and by beautiful things—just the very act of living, of walking and breathing and eating and having friends and chatting. Everything seems to look more beautiful rather than less, and one gets the much intensified sense of miracles.[3]

The ordinary as miraculous, seeing the marvelousness of all that is without the aid of magic enchantments, that is the inner freedom of those who have followed the way of Zen. No one has put it better than the haiku poets who, like Matsuo Basho, saw rich and universal, if almost inexpressible, significance in the most ordinary sights:

> On a withered branch
> a crow has settled—
> autumn nightfall.

Or this one, said to express the whole mystery of Buddhism to those who understand:

> An old pond
> a frog jumps in—
> the sound of water.

The famous Zen ox-herding pictures portray the passage from ordinary to enlightened consciousness through a series of paintings of a boy searching for a lost ox, which represents the Buddha-mind within all of us. Poems accompany each of the pictures. The richest and profoundest, to my mind, is the last. This lively picture portrays the ox-seeker and -finder, now an old man though a very wise child at heart, enlightened all the way down to the soles of his feet, clearly the elder in the Unitive state, walking—rather dancing—down the road on the way into the city "with bliss-bearing hands." As he goes he stops to play with children along the way, utterly unself-conscious about his dignity, clowning and laughing with them, his grin as wide as the full moon which symbolizes enlightenment. The verse says:

> Barefooted and naked of breast, I mingle
>     with the people of the world.
> My clothes are ragged and dust-laden,
>     and I am ever blissful.
> I use no magic to extend my life;
> Now, before me, the dead trees become alive.

Though there may be rills and rises even on plateaus, the dominant feature of the plateau or enlightenment or Unitive state is its deep-level steadiness when it is attained—post-mortem, in the wisdom of age. Perhaps its Unitive as well as plateau nature can be seen by thinking of it as an experience of no-self, in the very positive sense of being very much alive yet having transcended the ordinary finite self or ego to which we ordinarily cling, but whose moods come and go with winds of fear and desire. Maslow might not have used that particular language, but others have.

The contemporary mystic of the Unitive state, Bernadette Roberts, tells of how she came to realize she had no self—for her, of course, a positive discovery. For if you unite with God, the obverse of that is possessing no separate, individual self, for the *little* self is absorbed, lost, in the infinite divine self. But she did

not entirely understand what all this meant. The fol-
lowing incident occurred around the time of her trans-
formation:

> On my way to the library one afternoon, I
> stopped by Lucille's house to see if she might
> be taking her daily walk in my direction. While
> getting her things together she casually asked
> me, "So what's new?" I replied, "I don't have a
> self anymore." She turned to me with a bemused
> smile, "You, of all people! No self?" and broke
> into such a hearty laughter that I had to steady
> her on her feet. When she stopped laughing she
> asked, "Now tell me, seriously, what does this
> mean—you have no self?" I told her I didn't
> know, which was why I was on my way to the
> library, to find out. Then she began laughing all
> over again, and her laughter was infectious; after
> all, what could be more absurd than losing your
> self?
>
> As we walked along I told her about this
> unusual state and described some of its effects.
> At one point she stopped walking and turned
> to me, "You know," she said, "I recognize what
> you are describing, but I'm wondering how you
> know all this, because you are too young. What
> you are talking about is the aging process. It is
> change of consciousness that is reserved for the
> final years. It is the last stage in life, a getting
> ready for a new existence—and you're too
> young!"
>
> Since Lucille was eighty-five at the time, she
> was bewildered and a bit skeptical to find her
> experiences mirrored in a woman almost forty

years younger. She couldn't understand how this could be and, naturally, I didn't understand it myself. . . .

In the next two years of sharing this journey, we were repeatedly struck by the similarity of our experiences, by our individual but similar descriptions, and even by the similarity of the coping mechanisms we had devised in the process—she was continually giving me lessons on how to remember I was forgetful. She told me of her "compensations"—as she called the seeing of "It" which I called Oneness—and of the times she too, had "turned away" because of its overwhelming intensity. In the Passageway [equivalent to the Dark Night], where I felt myself to be walking on the brink of insanity, she thought of herself as walking on the "verge of senility." And where I felt my mind to be in a vise, she described it as a caul. Since it would be impossible to recount all of her experiences, let it suffice to say that almost step by step, what I have described of this journey belongs equally to Lucille.

If there was any noticeable difference, it was that her "self," as she told me, had gradually fallen away over a period of six years or more; it had not fallen away abruptly, as in my case. Also, our major concern or emphasis was different. From beginning to end, my concern was the mystery of what remained in the absence of self; whereas for Lucille, the mystery lay in just how much of her self she could live without. She never doubted for a moment, however, that when everything was gone, when everything had been

"shed," God would be all that remained . . .
[W]e were convinced we were sharing the great-
est, most important event of the human experi-
ence. Neither birth nor any experience up to this
time could hold a candle to the utter reality and
awesomeness of this final journey. In truth, this
is where life begins![4]

Little can be added to this account. It is time to
move on to that end which is also the beginning.

## Many Meetings, Many Partings:
### Circling Paths through Death and Life

I t is there, we know. Looking down, facing us, coming up from below, gnawing at us from within. Death. We try to deal with it all sorts of ways, play games with it. Pretend it isn't there. Pretend it is only something nice, covered with flowers and beautiful poetry, as at a funeral. Try to make sense of the old philosopher Epicurus' alleged indifference to it: "Where death is, I am not; where I am, death is not." Be stoic, be heroic, be sentimental, be philosophical and even theosophical. It doesn't go away. So over this final adversary and old friend each of us can only put what template for understanding we can. As Hamlet in his famous soliloquy says:

> But that the dread of something after death —
> The undiscover'd country, from whose bourn
> No traveler returns — puzzles the will,
> And makes us rather bear those ills we have
> Than fly to others that we know not of?

Yet few assertions from immortal literature are more egregiously in error than the lines declaring that this "undiscover'd country" is one from which no traveler has returned, if the testimony of most of the world's religions, and the testimony of thousands of individual experiencers, is to be believed. They say the country *has* been discovered, and the dark seas between there and here crossed not only one way, but both.

The annals of primal religion tell of shamans whose main vocation was to serve as a psychopomp or guide of the souls of those departing for the other shore, and who also knew of shortcuts by which the shaman could go there and return—as guide, as bearer of messages both ways, as retriever of strayed souls. The Eskimo shaman, we are told, received power in this manner and for these purposes:

> The *angákok* consists "of a mysterious light which the shaman suddenly feels in his body, inside his head, within the brain, an inexplicable searchlight, a luminous fire, which enables him to see in the dark, both literally and metaphorically speaking, for he can now, even with closed eyes, see through darkness and perceive things and coming events, which are hidden from others; thus they look into the future and into the secrets of others."

The candidate obtains this mystical light after long hours of waiting, sitting on a bench in his hut and invoking the spirits. When he experiences it for the first time "it is as if the house in which he is suddenly rises; he sees far ahead of him, through mountains, exactly as if the earth were one great plain, and his eyes could reach to the end of the earth. Nothing is hidden from him any longer; not only can he see things far, far away, but he can also discover souls, stolen souls, which are either kept concealed in far, strange lands, or have been taken up or down to the Land of the Dead."[1]

The shaman's implementation of this power is no less dramatic. Among the Salish Indians of the Pacific Northwest, for example, the shaman would go through an imaginary journey by water to recover the lost and stolen soul of a sick person. Together with a crew of ten other shamans, they would enact crossing the great sea separating our world from the Land of the Dead, making motions as though paddling, till finally they reached that half-undiscover'd country. Once there, the shamanic party had further obstacles to overcome: a raging torrent, conquered by laying a trunk across the river to serve as a bridge; a guardian who refused to tell them the way until they struggled with the guardian; and finally spirits (played by boys of the tribe) who would try to defend their country against the shamans' entry with burning torches. But finally the shamans would enter, find the sick person's soul, and then triumphantly return, singing the song of that soul. As one can well imagine, after seeing such a heroic journey made on the patient's behalf, and hearing the song of her or his own returning soul, the patient would be so moved that she or he would jump up and be cured.[2]

The Christian religion proclaims as its central message that at least one person, Jesus Christ, has returned from the dead to rise again in his physical body, after having also "visited the spirits in prison" (the "descent into hell"). Hinduism and Buddhism say that not just one has returned, but that all of us have experienced both birth and death many, many times, and will do so time and time again, until we are finally able to shuffle off for good that "mortal coil" of which Hamlet spoke, to become free of death, birth, and time.

Recently, much attention has been given to Near-Death Experiences (NDEs), first described under that name by Raymond Moody in his 1975 book, *Life After Life*. Moody found that a large number of people who have been close to clinical death, but have been revived, report remarkable experiences that share many common features. At first the person may just experience separation from the body. To their amazement, they may find themselves hovering in the air, looking down calmly from above or from near the ceiling of the hospital room on the devastated physical body. They may then see a powerful light, often resolving into a tunnel of light, down which they move. A benign figure may appear, called the "Being of Light" by Moody but often identified with Jesus, angels, or gods by religious persons. At this time they often see their entire lives in a flash—the "life review"—and sometimes not only their own lives but that of all those beings whom they have affected for good or ill. Seeing themselves in the presence of the overwhelming love of the Being of Light and in the profoundly meaningful world of light, and knowing how they have touched the lives of others, is enough to bring most voyagers beyond death to a deep awareness of themselves, faults and all.

At this point those who return to tell the story will be told their time has not yet come, or they will be given a choice. A few may journey so far as to see other beings on that farther shore, perhaps departed loved ones as a "welcoming party." They may even see the beautiful paradisal fields farther up and further in this land on the other side of the veil. The experiencers then return to the body, often deeply moved and changed by the experience, saying they no longer have any fear of death, having been there. Motivated to live spiritually and in love toward all beings in a new way, NDErs have been known to seem so different to their families and friends as virtually to be another person; this has caused consternation as well as rejoicing.

A significant minority of NDErs have also experienced negative aspects of the other side. While there are few reports reflecting the conventional hell, some have encountered impish or demonic entities, probably from the lower astral plane, who have taunted or tormented them, perhaps until dispersed by higher beings. Many have been confused at first, especially those who have suffered violent or unexpected death. It seems clear that the NDE world has several levels, and is experienced in different ways by different people.

None of this is anything new. The well-known *Tibetan Book of the Dead,* or *Bardo Thodol,* presents a picture which, though in Buddhist language, fits the near-death experience closely. It is basically an account of the experiences of the "soul" (technically the karmic energy-residue) after it leaves the physical body at the hour of death. According to the *Bardol Thodol,* during the forty-nine days of its transit from one embodied life to another, the soul experiences a series of remarkable visions which—if it recognizes them as projections of its own consciousness—it can unite with to find transcendent liberation. But if it shrinks from them, the soul continues on the path between the worlds until, propelled by the high winds of karma, it seeks a fresh womb here below, and the human odyssey of suffering and hope begins for it once more.

The Pilgrim in the *Tibetan Book of the Dead* commences, at the "highest" level suggestive of the NDE light experience, to encounter the "Clear Light of the Void." This clarity is of a terrifying brightness, and out of It comes a roaring that is louder than a thousand thunderclaps at once. It is the light and vibrancy of the entire cosmos put together. If, nonetheless, the voyager can recognize It as one with her or his own true nature, she or he can merge with it and attain supreme liberation, being united with the universal Essence beyond all duality. Most travelers to this half-discovered country, though, will find the brightness and the loudness too powerful for their spiritual eyes and ears, and will instinctively shrink back, the priceless moment of opportunity lost.

But there are fresh opportunities. The entity next faces, one at a time and then all together, a mandala of five great cosmic buddhas in their "peaceful" aspects. They are like heavenly forms of the universal Reality. If the entity recognizes any or all of them as projections of her or his own true nature, unification occurs and thus liberation from returning; if they are not recognized for what they are, the entity passes on and continues the Pilgrimage.

Next the traveler encounters the same deities in their terrifying aspect: full of wrath, eyes bulging and tongue hanging out to lap the blood of victims as only the Tibetan imagination can conceive them, the fierceness of absolute truth against the errors and compromises of this world. But if the Pilgrim has the courage to recognize that these too are projections of her or his own nature, unification occurs, and thus salvation.

If even this is not enough, the forces leading to rebirth now take on greater and greater power. The Pilgrim may have flash visions of her or his judgment, and of future parents in physical union. Finally the Pilgrim swoons, and forgetting on the conscious level what has just been gone through, awakens in the womb of whatever human or animal, god or demon, is fated to give the traveler an upcoming life.

Even in the last stages of reentry, however, the Pilgrim can, with tremendous spiritual effort, cut short or redirect the process. The most effective means is meditation on the "father-mother guru," the image of a chosen deity or spiritual teacher in the *yabyum* posture, that is—with the explicitness of Tibet's Tantric art—ecstatically united with a female figure representing *prajña* or universal wisdom. In a characteristically bold and profound way, this mental image is portraying that the greatest power comes from the union of opposites, of which the union of male and female is the most potent symbol. The *Tibetan Book of the Dead* says that the dualism that leads to attachment and suffering in human life begins in the womb or in infancy, with the male-child's attachment to the mother and revulsion toward the father, and the opposite on the part of the female. Thus, a thousand years before Freud, the subjective power of the Oedipus complex was recognized. But by meditating effectively on one's image of spiritual guidance as bringing both together, this fatal polarity can be overcome. Then, with a shout of awakening, one can be born a marvelous and eternal child of both parents.

The traditional theosophical view of life after death is quite compatible with the NDE, as it is with the strikingly similar scenarios presented by earlier teachings such as those of Swedenborg and Spiritualism. It also has much in common with those of the Eastern religions behind the *Tibetan Book of the Dead,* if the prospect of reincarnation coming after the vistas of life on the other side is also added in, as it would be by most Theosophists. The theosophical view also depends on the concept of the several parts of human nature, presented earlier in this book. Here is the gist of this process: [3]

First the etheric body leaves the physical frame. This is the "etheric double" comprised of subtle matter, perhaps something like the electromagnetic "aura" captured by Kirlian photography. It forms a pattern for the physical form. The etheric "body" carries with it all of the "higher" or still more subtle-matter "bodies"—the astral, mental, intuitional, and divine. This etheric body is what may float up to the top of the room, and act just like the physical body except outside of its material constraints. But the etheric double dissolves within a few hours.

Then the astral body, and the higher components carried within it, is free to move into the astral plane, sometimes called the Kamaloka, or desire realm. It is a state of thought and feeling; what one desires appears before one, with all the liquid plasticity of the thought/feeling medium, and without physical stability. Imagine that you could no sooner think of the most ravishingly beautiful valley imaginable than you would be walking through it, in astral virtual reality. You would think of music to go with this paradise, and no sooner

would it be thought than, as in some cinematic extrav-
aganza, its melodies would be resounding through the
glade as you walk.

But then let fear or base passion arise out of some
cellar of your mind, and it also appears as no less real:
a snarling tiger barring the path, or a face coarse with
lust leering toward you. Over and over again, thoughts
and their outward mirrors rise and fall till your mind
reels, tires, and the images finally begin to fade. You
realize they are no more than dream images, like most
of what moves in our minds, and also no less than
them.

On the astral plane, desires—including angers and
hatreds and fears, also desires in the sense that we
become very attached to them—will therefore work
themselves out until exhausted. A person who was
much attached to fantasies of the material things of this
world may find the astral plane a purgatory or hell,
since he or she will suffer relentless desires which now
cannot be fulfilled. Without a physical body, angers
and hungers can only boil and bubble in frustration
until their energy finally subsides. Some say that such
an entity may try to fulfill such appetites vicariously
through others still in the flesh. Those given to drink,
or rather the idea of drink, try to possess drunkards,
and like parasites, share in the unrefined pleasures
of their hosts; those given to lust become leeches to
lechers.

All this is life on the lower astral plane, and has been
encountered by some NDErs. Some deceased persons,
known as "earthbound" spirits, find it hard to leave
their old haunts even for the lower astral realm, and
strive to linger long around them. Stories of ghosts may

be based on psychic perception of these slaves to the past and its places, though often such pitiful beings are not even full astral entities, but robot-like shells of etheric or astral material that has not completely dissolved.

A person who has managed to move her or his focus toward more aesthetic or loving pleasures will, however, find the astral plane a time of rest and growth and delight. For them it gives opportunity for great creativity and joy. One could create the most beautiful palaces imaginable, and share them with others, or fulfill one's richest dreams of achievement in art, music, or science. For the material of the astral realm easily becomes what is wished for through the power of thought alone. While some may make desire-objects which then enslave them, or which reflect enslavements never overcome, the truly creative person will find opportunities for expression previously only encountered in dreams—which are often simply a confused brief movement into the astral realm during sleep —and imagination. Eventually all these dreams, high and low, restful and zestful, must have an end. The purpose of the astral plane is to bring them to an end, and with them the timespan, and the lifetime, one concert of such dreams has created. As Hotspur says in Shakespeare's *Henry IV*, "But thought's the slave of life, and life time's fool; And time, that takes survey of all the world, Must have a stop." This is not, however, an ultimate end, though it may be of temporal dream and memory.

Basically, the purpose of the astral realm in the great Pilgrimage is purgation—to help the Pilgrim disassociate from a desire nature linked to a particular physical world experience, in order ultimately to continue the Pilgrimage in another time, place, and physical vehicle. This will obviously take shorter or longer depending on how deeply ingrained the desires are, and how low or high on the spectrum of the astral realm they are. Figures of twenty to forty years have been postulated, but of course it is hard to say how such spans correlate to earthly calendars. In any case, eventually the astral energies wear down even the most hardened cases, and the entity rises to higher levels.

When the astral energies have been exhausted and their lessons learned, the entity falls into a sleep which Helena Blavatsky referred to as the "second death." Time (as we have known it) stops. The astral sheath then falls away and dissolves, and one awakens to a much greater life than that of the astral plane, life in heaven or what Theosophy calls *Devachan*. With the physical, etheric, and astral sheaths left behind, what is left is the divine Trinity plus the intuitional and mental vehicles. This new realm, near to the divine light within, is built of pure thought untouched by feeling. Here the mind finds deep yet creative relaxation. Its thoughts may be formed or formless, but are on levels almost unimaginable to us now. We can imagine, though, that Devachan gives the mind a chance to fully explore and understand all the deepest impulses of its past life, and to get in touch with one's highest, least selfish ideas. If all goes well, these will be the seed-thoughts of one's creativity in the next physical incarnation.

For eventually the Devachan entity will desire to move toward rebirth and the adventure of new experience. Rest and detachment from the specifics of the last life will have been completed. Once again the entity will move into the stream of karma, and be propelled toward a womb whither it leads. That karma may, of course, include relationships with other entities that are connected to one's highest and most idealistic self. A poem by Rupert Brooke suggests awakening out of that Devachanic sleep at the summons of a connection forged by destiny and love:

> Out of the nothingness of sleep,
> The slow dreams of Eternity,
> There was a thunder on the deep:
> I came, because you called to me.
>
> I broke the Night's primeval bars,
> I dared the old abysmal curse,
> And flashed through ranks of frightened stars
> Suddenly on the universe!
>
> The eternal silences were broken;
> Hell became Heaven as I passed. —
> What shall I give you as a token,
> A sign that we have met, at last?
>
> I'll break and forge the stars anew,
> Shatter the heavens with a song;
> Immortal in my love for you,
> Because I love you, very strong . . . [4]

Greatly advanced souls may be able to make a conscious choice of the next birth, but most will simply be blown by winds of karma generated in a past life they have now consciously forgotten. What they carry over is not actual memories, no more than an actual body, but a mental nature whose style, character, and seed-potentialities have been shaped through the long incubation of Devachan. Out of this comes a new unique person in a new age probably very different from the one that went before.

People ask if you are going to heaven or hell. Theosophists say we have all been to both innumerable times, and probably will again, as we move around and around through the astral plane, Devachan, and the physical world, over and over until all lessons are learned and all potentialities realized—until we have been everything we can be that is good and latent in the nature of this particular Pilgrim. Embodied life is a long, long process of manifestation and withdrawal. You might ask why this is necessary. Why must we go through the traumas of birth and death over and over? Could not nature be arranged in such a way that an organism could simply regenerate itself until the end of time, without dying?

Perhaps. But the process would not be serving, as physical life should, the higher purpose of life, which is to enable the Pilgrim's journey through space and time back to the One. That journey requires that we know how to experience and then how to withdraw, how to attach and detach, how to be born and how to die. This we do over and over—and some day, as we approach the Final Forest before the lights and high towers of our ultimate Home, we will get it right.

What does all of this mean for our lives *now*? Sometimes not much. Admittedly, we have to do many ordinary, everyday tasks that would presumably be the same whether we had one life or many. In those moments we may be inclined to say, One life at a time. But that sardonically smiling visage, the death's head with which we began this chapter, is still there. Better to look death in the eye and smile back.

But how do we prepare for death as a part—a repeated part—of the journey along the Path? First, we can strengthen the timeless in ourselves now. Meditate. Love all that is beautiful, in art or music or nature, for it is the shadow of eternity. Above all, love others who are also timeless deep within, and are companions on the Pilgrimage as it wends its way beyond the circles of one lifetime. Some may be, for you, long-term, many lifetime companions; others may be fellow-wayfarers for a brief stretch of road only. Either way, they are reminders of the journey and its joys. For all are moving along, and no one is only what she or he now seems. We are full of secrets, even to ourselves till we become quite wise. As Æ wrote of Irish peasants, and alluding to the parable of the prodigal son:

> The gods have taken alien shapes upon them,
> Wild peasants driving swine
> In a strange country. Through the swarthy faces
> The starry faces shine.
>
> Under grey tattered skies they strain and reel there:
> Yet cannot all disguise
> The majesty of fallen gods, the beauty,
> The fire beneath their eyes.
>
> The huddle at night within low, clay built cabins;
> And, to themselves unknown,
> They carry with them diadem and sceptre
> And move from throne to throne.[5]

We are all kings, gods, pilgrims, actors playing many parts upon many stages, prodigal sons exiled to the pig-fields and reduced to eating the husks that the swine did eat, yet also wanderers in realms of gold. But the point is not to pride or pity ourselves on our noble birth and strange destiny, but rather to see the same in others. For we live not for ourselves alone but with others, and we will not truly find within ourselves that which we do not first see mirrored in another's eyes.

Realizations like these will help on the astral plane, for they strengthen that which responds to the higher astral realm of beneficent signs and love-shaped visions, while weakening attachment to the lower and earthbound parts of one's character. For such meditations affirm that which abides. If we can see that we, and all persons and objects, change but do not die, we see also that it is pointless to hold with either craving or hatred particular scenes or faces on the screen. Let it go, rise up, move on.

Also, understand the choices you have about dying. Older spiritual books and teachers both Eastern and Western have, like the *Tibetan Book of the Dead,* emphasized the importance of a "good death." They have made it seem that it is very much your own choice whether you die confessing your sins, forgiving your enemies, and commending your soul to God, or to the Buddhas in the Bardo realm of the Tibetan schema. For all its good intentions, such instruction has undoubtedly created no small amount of unnecessary guilt and anxiety, for owing to the uncertainties of illness and violence we may not be able to fully control our state of mind at death, just as we cannot fully determine the physical time and place of the departure. I assume we will be judged, or our karma will respond, in relation to the pattern of an entire life and its dominant tendencies, not solely to the moment which happens chronologically to be the last. Yet spiritually the point is well taken. For there are choices we can make. They are not necessarily choices about the last minute only, for that may well be indeterminate; they are choices about the character of a lifetime which if consistently followed will in the nature of things govern the final hours as they have all the rest of the life.

We can therefore decide such issues as whether we will die alone, or recognize that—whether physically or spiritually—we are surrounded by others. For this is really a question of how much we always try to realize that we live not alone, but in love and peace, so much as in us lies, with all beings. We can decide in what state of mind we will die. While we may not be able to control mental deprivation induced by illness or medicine, we can decide now, by the character of our life and attitude, whether we will die suicidal, drugged, drunk, or angry—all of which are likely to influence negatively the astral plane experience. Subconscious suicidalism, expressed through recklessness with sex, tobacco, drink, violence, or self-neglect—read self-hatred—will have results little different than the actual act itself. All of this is within our power to control now. We can decide now also what spiritual attitude we are going to take to death, and try to hold the fears, anxieties—and half-conscious death wishes—accountable to our life beyond the present. Finally, we can decide where we are going with our death. We can think past the astral realm, although it would not hurt to have some ideas in preparation for it about what kind of astral experiences we will build for ourselves.

We can also think forward to the mental realm and Devachan. The details must wait, but you can be thinking about the seed-motif you will plant in that unimaginably inward garden, to blossom in another lifetime far in the esoteric future. What is your best dream for serving the world? What work of art best epitomizes who you are at the very highest? What is the core or essence of that dream and that image? Dwell on these things and build them up as you go toward death. The effort will not be wasted.

To be sure, back on the earth-plane, these preparations are not always easy to remember, though it can get easier to do so. But even when we are grimly slogging through the underbrush of space and time, it sometimes helps to get just a glimpse of something beyond our current focus. A trail winding through the mountains may for long be so closed in by trees and rocks as to be almost like walking through urban canyons lined with storefronts, when suddenly you break onto a high pass, and there are ranges upon ranges of snowy mountains, forever forests running to the sky, and infinite blue above. Then that is enough to get you breathing again, and to realize that even the dimmest passages of the trail lead toward infinite horizons. Even when the view is cloaked in fog, and only enough is visible to reveal there is sunlight past the mists and here and there a bit of trail, you want to go on.

You call to your companions, for one of the strangest mysteries of such vistas of natural beauty is that they evoke a sense you have seen it before, with others who are dear to you. You feel, then, or after thinking it over later, that we are trailmates who have walked together in the past, and will meet again on future voyages between the centuries and the worlds. We are drawn together by deep affinities. Often we think not consciously of such things, for on much of life's trail one step at a time is enough, just as we do not always see even those we love most as timeless and immortal kings and queens of faery realms, though they are that too. But we also know we are with them, and though at times those forms and eyes may be cloaked and veiled, we will see the splendor of the stars once again in their faces. As John Henry Newman wrote:

> Lead, Kindly Light, amid the encircling gloom,
>   Lead Thou me on!
> The night is dark, and I am far from home—
>   Lead Thou me on!
> Keep Thou my feet; I do not ask to see
>   The distant scene—one step enough for me.
>
> I was not ever thus, nor prayed that Thou
>   Shouldest lead me on.
> I loved to choose and see my path; but now
>   Lead Thou me on!
> I loved the garish day, and, spite of fears,
> Pride ruled my will; remember not past years.
>
> So long Thy power hath blessed me, sure it still
>   Will lead me on,
> O'er moor and fen, o'er crag and torrent, till
>   The night is gone;
> And with the morn those angel faces smile
> Which I have loved long since, and lost awhile.

If something in your soul responds to such vistas, and you cannot help but feel there is more to life than the surface of our present days and years—

You are part of the hidden brotherhood.
You are one with all the wise, all true seekers,
    and all theosophists in this and all other
    worlds strewn throughout the sea of stars.
You are on the Path.

## Always Beginning,
## Always Coming Home

The trip through life we are on is a peculiar one, unlike any other, in that the place of setting out and the final destination can seem far, impossibly and unimaginably far away, most of the time. And yet, whenever you really want to, you can step off the Path to go back and revisit the nursery where you began, or climb up some high cliff to catch at least a glimpse of the Halls of Light where you will receive your final welcome. For it is a trip that is what you make it to be, and does not go by the ordinary rules.

There are moments when we feel fresh and eager, as though life were just about to begin, and we look enthusiastically down the long vista of the future. And there are other times when with unitive calm we seem to be fulfilled right where we are, as though the journey were not really going somewhere so much as circling around and around something that is always there, and is of far greater worth than anything east of the sun or west of the moon. Both times are good. Indeed, all times are good to those on the Path, even those which offer painful trials, just as for those who truly love seasons there are equal but different beauties in spring, summer, autumn, and winter.

Where we go on the Path is not necessarily toward greater factual knowledge about sacred things, for all one can do with words is point toward that which is far beyond the grasp of any human language, like the Zen finger pointing at the moon. One can point with sophisticated philosophical vocabularies, with the crude but heartfelt tongue of a deprived child like Pharoah on his pitiful swatch of peaceful grass, or with the nonverbal symbols of religions, from those of the Stone Age to those of the great cathedrals of Europe and temples of Asia. Always one is pointing far beyond oneself, and in the end the words one is able to use bespeak more one's culture and education than the true secrets and yearnings of the spiritual heart.

Nor does walking the Path mean walking closer to God or Ultimate Reality, for the Absolute is already everywhere. One can get no closer to it than one is right now, for it is the essence and innermost nature of all that is, has always been and will always be, including you and me.

Rather, we are back to where we were at the start of the pilgrimage of this book: that the real growth is growth in awareness. Awareness is a little different from knowledge, or from spatial nearness. Awareness is a combination of seeing, feeling, and knowing—all, of course, with the inner senses as well as the outer. It is perceiving, say, an animal in the zoo, or a household pet, and registering at once both its beauty and its inwardness, what it is feeling and thinking. This will require a flash of complete attention and of inner openness to full awareness, both at once.

When that double watchfulness is directed, like a pair of binoculars, on the divine or on that within our lives which moves us toward alignment with the divine work in ourselves and the world, we move significantly along the Path. Methods of worship, prayer and meditation help; so do those acts of kindness and charity which sensitize ourselves even as they help others; so do simple seeing, loving, and reflecting.

Moving significantly along the Path? As we have noted, spiritual "progress" is far more subtle a thing than getting degrees or merit badges, or even of making headway down the road in your car. It is perhaps more comparable to the kind of "growth" you can attain in good counseling or psychotherapy sessions, but even that is not quite it. If you can imagine an inner eye watching you from within as you change and grow through therapy, and in the process quietly waxing in awareness of yourself, the world, and God, that would be more like it.

Awareness can of course be retained, and one can become more and more habituated to the wisdom attitudes of mind and loving patterns of behavior that are one and the same in true awareness. For with awareness one comes to a profound sense of the pity and sentience and interrelatedness and imperishable sacredness of all that is; this is wisdom, and the only possible ethical expression of such wisdom is love or compassion. No one begins to have real wisdom or awareness who does not so demonstrate it.

Yet to grow in awareness and love is not to go into automatic pilot—always and effortlessly doing the right and the true. We have observed that spirituality is far more an art than an assembly-line process. There may be acquired skills and perceptions, yet it always is the labor of the day, it always requires deep attention, and the mightiest struggles may come (the Dark Night . . .) after one has well begun. One's spiritual journey is rarely perfect, especially as one's own awareness increases and with it the standards one tries to apply to oneself. All this is comparable to the burdens borne by great artists and other creative persons.

Yet, keep on going. There are two consolations. One, if our perspective is correct, this is a journey of far more than one lifetime or one world. That makes it exciting, for there will be much to see and do. It is also encouraging, for it tells us that more time than the short present span from cradle to grave awaits us, to uproot all our ignorance and all our faults. And we know ourselves well enough to know it may take more time—much more time. But that is no reason for slacking, for all true advance on the Path will be carried over. If in the elder years we really come near the Unitive state, the next sunrise will be bright indeed.

The second consolation is knowing that there is help. Helping hands reach down to gently guide us or even pull us along the way, especially in the rough parts. All the great religions assure us that God's grace or power is there to aid us, often even before we ask. Many tell us also that heaven and earth are filled with intermediate helpers on the spiritual side as well, with face and form one can visualize: saints, angels, gods, bodhisattvas, kindly spirits great and small. Theosophy tells us there are Mahatmas or Masters both in the flesh of this world and on the inner planes prepared to assist with wisdom and power those who open themselves to them. They are on the Path like ourselves, but a bit farther ahead, and able to look back toward us with strong and encouraging eyes. Finally, there are guides visible all around us: gurus, teachers, pastors, elders, friends—whoever we know and trust, whether far advanced or only a little more so than us—who can help with both words and silences, with counsel and prayer, or with a warm smile and a helping hand.

You are already on the Path. Look around, see where it lies, and view the lay of the land through which it winds. Today is a good day for hiking. First sit down, plan out what you need to take and pack your spiritual knapsack; mentally lay it out and organize it. Stay there till you are calm, centered, and able to see far. Then get up and start Walking, inwardly if not literally. Bless all the plants and animals you see, smile at the first person you meet, and adjust your inner eyes for distance and up-close awareness.

# Notes

## 1  A SERIES OF SUNRISES

1.  Helena P. Blavatsky, *The Secret Doctrine*. Wheaton, IL: Theosophical Publishing House, Quest Edition, 1993, vol. I, p. 329.

## 2  CHINKS OF ETERNITY

1.  Rupert Brooke, "Dining-Room Tea," *The Collected Poems of Rupert Brooke*. New York: Dodd, Mead, 1915, 1943, pp. 86–87.

2.  Swami Prabhavananda and Christopher Isherwood, transl., *The Song of God: Bhagavad-Gita*. New York: Mentor Books, 1954, p. 67.

3.  Evelyn Underhill, *Mysticism: A Study in the Nature and Development of Man's Spiritual Consciousness*. London: Methuen, 1911.

## 3  WAKE OF SPLENDOR: INFANCY AND CHILDHOOD

1.  Edward Hoffman, *Visions of Innocence: Spiritual and Inspirational Experiences of Childhood*. Boston: Shambhala Press, 1992, pp. 26–27.

2. Ibid., p. 18.

3. Alex Kotlowitz, *There Are No Children Here: The Story of Two Boys Growing Up in the Other America*. New York: Doubleday, 1991.

4. Robert Coles, *The Spiritual Life of Children*. Boston: Houghton Mifflin, 1990, p. 142.

5. Anne Frank, *The Diary of Anne Frank*. New York: Doubleday, 1952, 1967, p. 189. First published in Dutch in 1947.

6. Aldous Huxley, *Heaven and Hell*. New York: Harper & Brothers, 1956.

7. Alison Lurie, *Don't Tell the Grown-Ups: Why Kids Love the Books They Do*. New York: Avon, 1990.

8. Kelly Bulkeley, "Psychological and Spiritual Development in Childhood," *Religious Studies Review*, 21/2, April 1995, p. 88.

9. Mircea Eliade, *Autobiography, vol. I, 1907-1937: Journey East, Journey West*. San Francisco: Harper & Row, 1981, pp. 6–7.

## 4 QUESTING AND NESTING: ADLOESCENCE AND YOUNG ADULTHOOD

1. The following poems are from Æ, *Voices of the Stones*. London: Macmillan, 1925, pp. 21, 31, 39.

## 5 THE SUN IN STRENGTH: THE YEARS OF EARLY CREATIVITY

1. Swami Prabhavananda and Frederick Manchester, trans., *The Upanishads*. New York: Mentor Books, 1948, pp. 27–28.

2. Richard Maurice Bucke, *Cosmic Consciousness*. New Hyde Park, NY: University Books, 1961, pp. 7—8. Originally pub. 1901.

## 6 THE DEMONS AND DELIGHTS OF MIDDAY: MIDDLE AGE

1. Evelyn Underhill, *Mysticism,* p. 457.

2. Cited in Andreas Lommel, *Shamanism: The Beginnings of Art*. New York: McGraw-Hill, 1967, p. 29.

3. Swami Prabhavananda and Frederick Manchester, trans. *The Upanishads: Breath of the Eternal*. New York: Mentor Books, 1948, 1957, pp. 120—21.

4. Helen Waddell, *The Desert Fathers*. Ann Arbor: University of Michigan Press, 1957, p. 35.

## 7 SUNSET AND EVENING STAR: THE BEAUTY OF OLD AGE

1. Cited in Tom S. Cleary and Sam I. Shapiro, "The Plateau Experience and the Post-Mortem Life: Abraham H. Maslow's Unfinished Theory," *The Journal of Transpersonal Psychology* 27, 1 (November 1995), p. 2.

2. Edward Hoffman, *The Right to Be Human: A Biography of Abraham Maslow*. Los Angeles: Tarcher, 1988, p. 340.

3. Cited in Cleary and Shapiro, "The Plateau Experience," p. 19.

4. Bernadette Roberts, *The Experience of No-Self*. Boston: Shambhala, 1982, pp. 193—95.

## 8    MANY MEETINGS, MANY PARTINGS: CIRCLING PATHS THROUGH DEATH AND LIFE

1. Mircea Eliade, *Shamanism: Archaic Techniques of Ecstasy,* Bollengen Series LXXVI. New York: Pantheon Books, 1964, pp. 60–61. Quoted material from Knud Rasmussen, *Intellectual Culture of the Iglulik Eskimos.* Copenhagen, 1930, pp. 112–13.

2. Andreas Lommel, *Shamanism: The Beginning of Art.* New York: McGraw-Hill, 1967, p. 97.

3. This account is based on my writings in Robert Ellwood, *Theosophy.* Wheaton, IL: Theosophical Publishing House, 1986, pp. 108–14. It should be noted that some differences in terminology and detail appear in various theosophical sources.

4. Rupert Brooke, "The Call," *The Collected Poems of Rupert Brooke.* New York: Dodd, Mead, 1915, 1943, p. 40.

5. George Russell (Æ), "Exiles," *Voices of the Stones.* London: Macmillan, 1925, p. 2.